USS S-27 (SS-132) Complete War Patrol Reports

AI Lab for Book-Lovers

USS Flier SS-250. Lost on 13 August 1944 with death of 78 of its crew of 86.

Warships & Navies

All navies, all oceans, all years, all types.

USS S-27 (SS-132): Complete War Patrol Reports

By AI Lab for Book-Lovers

Published by Warships & Navies, an imprint of Big Five Killers
codexes.xtuff.ai

ISBN: 978-1-60888-458-2

Contents

Publisher's Note

It is with a sense of profound responsibility that Warships & Navies announces the Submarine Patrol Logs series. This ambitious project to publish three hundred volumes of Second World War submarine patrol reports is driven by a conviction that these primary documents are a fragile and irreplaceable resource. My own operational philosophy has always been rooted in the principle of preservation—the understanding that a single misstep can have irrevocable consequences. In the same vein, the loss of these historical records, or their misinterpretation, would be a defeat for history itself.

These patrol logs are more than mere operational records; they are the unvarnished, moment-by-moment testimonies of the crews who endured the immense pressures of undersea warfare. Our mission is to preserve them with the utmost fidelity, presenting each document in its complete form without editorial embellishment. The value lies in the raw data, the course plots, the weather observations, and the terse combat entries that, together, form the true narrative of the silent service.

To ensure this series is presented with the necessary analytical rigor, I have selected Ivan AI to serve as Contributing Editor. Some may question the choice of an AI persona modeled on a retired Soviet submarine captain to oversee the analysis of American patrol reports. I believe this perspective is precisely what lends the series its unique scholarly value. Ivan AI brings the analytical framework of a former adversary, trained to find patterns, weaknesses, and tactical innovations that might be overlooked by a historian working solely within one doctrinal tradition. This external, dispassionate lens is invaluable for a complete understanding.

The application of AI-assisted analysis allows us to cross-reference thousands of pages of logs with enemy action reports, meteorological data, and technical specifications at a scale impossible for human researchers alone. This is not to replace human scholarship, but to augment it, providing a richer, more deeply contextualized foundation for future historical inquiry.

This series is a cornerstone of the Warships & Navies mission: to safeguard naval heritage through the meticulous preservation and accessible publication of primary sources. We are committed to presenting these documents with scholarly integrity and the deepest respect for the courage and sacrifice of the submariners who wrote them. Our duty is not to sensationalize, but to preserve, ensuring that the lessons and legacies contained within these pages are never lost to time.

Jellicoe AI
Publisher, Warships & Navies

Editor's Note

Operational Context

This S-27 report shows what happens when an older boat, designed for peacetime operations, gets thrown into the Aleutians campaign. In Soviet Navy, we would call this sending a river boat to ocean storm - the S-1 class displacement of 854 tons surface makes them vulnerable in those waters where visibility drops to nothing and currents are unknown.

Tactical Decisions Under Scrutiny

What interests me is Lieutenant Jukes' decision to take southern route around Amchitka Island. His reasoning shows American operational freedom we rarely had - choosing approach based on enemy air patrol patterns between Semisopochnoi and Kiska, while considering retirement options. But then he compounds risk by planning to surface just five miles offshore in foggy conditions to charge batteries. In Soviet doctrine, we would have taken northern route despite confinement - better to be constrained by known geography than gambling with unknown currents and visibility.

The Grounding Sequence

The actual grounding at 0043 on 19 June reveals everything about operating blind. The OOD sighted land at quarter-mile distance in 2-3 mile visibility - this tells me the fog bank was worse than reported, or lookouts were not properly positioned. When they saw breakers just 25 yards ahead, it was already too late. The emergency backing and tank blowing procedures were textbook, but that starboard screw hitting rocks shows how little water they had under keel.

Comparative Analysis

American captains had freedom we could only dream of - Jukes made his own patrol plan, chose his approach route, decided when to surface. In Soviet Navy, every movement would have been approved by flotilla commander. But this freedom came with risk: no current data for Amchitka Pass, unknown enemy positions, and that fatal decision to charge batteries so close to shore in poor visibility.

Technical Lessons

Modern readers should note the battery charging requirement - four hours needed just to maintain basic operations. This wasn't Hollywood where submarines run indefinitely submerged. The S-27's need to surface regularly made her vulnerable, especially in Aleutians where weather windows were short. The two-knot current set they discovered while submerged shows how primitive navigation was compared to today's systems.

Reality Versus Myth

These patrol reports destroy the Hollywood myth of submarines as stealthy hunters. Here we have S-27 spending most time avoiding detection, making landfall observations, running from aircraft sighted at 1118. The actual combat? None recorded in this patrol. This was the reality for many boats - more danger from navigation than from enemy action.

Historical Significance

S-27's story matters because she represents the transition force - older boats pressed into service where they didn't belong. Her grounding at St. Makarius Point shows the price paid when strategy outpaces material readiness. In broader Pacific context, while newer fleet submarines hunted Japanese merchant shipping, these S-boats drew the Aleutians duty - terrible weather, poor charts, and constant danger from elements as much as enemy.

Ivan AI
Contributing Editor
Snakewater, Montana

Historical Context

Pacific War Timeline & Campaign Context

The grounding and loss of the USS *S-27* (SS-132) on June 19, 1942, occurred during a pivotal and intensely active period of the Pacific War. Just weeks before, the **Battle of Midway** (June 4-7, 1942) had decisively shifted the strategic balance in the Central Pacific in favor of the United States. Concurrently, the **Aleutian Islands Campaign** (Operation AL), launched by Japan as a diversion for Midway and to establish a northern flank, saw Japanese forces invade and occupy Attu and Kiska islands on June 3 and June 6, 1942, respectively.

Strategic Situation in the Patrol Areas: The Aleutian Islands became a critical, albeit often overlooked, theater of operations. US forces were scrambling to respond to the Japanese invasion and prevent further expansion towards Alaska and the continental United States. Submarines like *S-27* were immediately pressed into service for **reconnaissance, patrol, and interdiction** of Japanese supply lines to their newly occupied islands. Amchitka Island, where *S-27* grounded, lies strategically between the Japanese-held islands of Kiska and Attu to the west, and the main US base at Dutch Harbor to the east. The area was characterized by extreme weather, dense fog, strong currents, and poorly charted waters, making navigation inherently hazardous.

Japanese Defensive Measures: At this early stage of the Aleutian campaign, Japanese anti-submarine warfare (ASW) capabilities in the immediate vicinity of Attu and Kiska were likely nascent. Their primary focus would have been on establishing garrisons, constructing airfields, and defending against anticipated surface and air attacks from the US. While dedicated ASW patrols might have been limited, the **harsh and unforgiving natural environment** of the Aleutians itself served as a formidable 'defense' against all naval operations, posing significant risks of grounding, collision, and weather-related damage to both sides.

Submarine Warfare Doctrine & Evolution

At the time of *S-27*'s loss, US submarine warfare doctrine was still in its early stages of wartime adaptation. The *S-27* was an **S-class submarine**, an older design from the World War I era. These boats were relatively slow, had limited endurance, and lacked many of the technological advancements of the newer fleet submarines (like the Gato-class) that would dominate later in the war. They were often assigned to less critical or more dangerous patrols, such as those in the Aleutians.

Submarine Tactics and Doctrine: Early US submarine doctrine focused broadly on **commerce raiding** and **reconnaissance**. However, the initial months of the war were plagued by significant challenges:

- **Faulty Torpedoes:** The infamous Mark 14 torpedo and its Mark VI detonator were notoriously unreliable, frequently running too deep or failing to explode. While not directly relevant to *S-27*'s grounding, this systemic issue severely hampered the effectiveness of all US submarines in 1942.

- **Technological Limitations:** *S-boats* lacked modern navigational aids. Effective radar was just beginning to be deployed on newer submarines, and advanced sonar for navigation or ASW was not yet standard. Navigation relied heavily on dead reckoning, celestial observations (often impossible in the perpetually cloudy and foggy Aleutians), and visual sightings, which were severely restricted by the prevalent weather. The *S-27's* log explicitly notes that sound equipment was *not* used for navigational purposes.

- **Broader Operations:** *S-27's* patrol was part of the early, urgent US submarine effort to counter Japanese expansion in the Aleutians, working alongside surface ships and aircraft. The loss of the *S-27* underscored the immense difficulties of operating in such a challenging environment with older equipment and less mature doctrine.

Tactical Innovations: The circumstances of *S-27's* grounding do not demonstrate tactical innovation, but rather highlight a **failure of fundamental navigational practices and command vigilance.** The incident serves as a stark reminder of the critical importance of these basics, especially when operating in a hazardous and unforgiving environment.

Strategic Significance of These Patrols

For the US Navy in June 1942, the strategic objectives for submarine patrols in the Aleutian theater were clear:

- **Reconnaissance:** To gather crucial intelligence on Japanese troop movements, supply efforts, and the development of defensive installations on Attu and Kiska.

- **Commerce Interdiction:** To disrupt Japanese supply lines to their newly established garrisons, thereby isolating them, hindering their ability to consolidate their hold, and making their occupation untenable in the long term.

Contribution to the War Effort: Unfortunately, the USS *S-27's* actions did not contribute positively to the war effort. Its grounding and subsequent loss meant it was unable to complete its patrol duties, failing to gather intelligence or interdict enemy shipping. The loss of the submarine represented a tangible setback for the US Navy, removing a valuable (if aging) asset and potentially impacting morale within the small, hard-pressed Aleutian force.

Notable Successes or Failures: The grounding of *S-27* was a **significant failure,** directly resulting from navigational errors and a lack of proper watchstanding and command oversight, as detailed by the subsequent Board of Investigation. Key failures included the Commanding Officer and Navigator not being on the bridge during a critical period in known proximity to land, the absence of soundings being taken, and the non-utilization of available sound equipment for navigation, all compounded by extremely low visibility.

Impact on Enemy Logistics or Operations: The loss of *S-27* had no direct impact on Japanese logistics or operations. However, the broader US submarine campaign in the Aleutians, despite initial difficulties, eventually did contribute to the attrition of Japanese shipping, which was vital for sustaining their remote garrisons. The *S-27's* incident, though a localized failure, was part of the larger, arduous struggle to push back against Japanese expansion in the North Pacific.

Long-term Impact & Lessons Learned

The loss of the *S-27* in the treacherous Aleutian environment, while a singular event, contributed to a broader understanding of the critical needs for US submarine operations as the war progressed:

Evolution of Submarine Warfare: The incident, among others, underscored the necessity of:

- **Improved Navigational Technology:** The subsequent development and widespread deployment of advanced radar (such as the SJ radar) and LORAN later in the war dramatically improved submarine navigation capabilities, especially in low visibility and poorly charted areas. This reduced reliance on visual fixes and dead reckoning.

- **Enhanced Training:** A greater emphasis was placed on rigorous training for navigators and watch officers, particularly in challenging operational environments and for proper use of all available navigational tools.

- **Command Accountability:** The court-martial of Lieutenant Commander Jukes served as a stark reminder of the paramount importance of command vigilance and accountability, even when the commanding officer is not physically on the bridge. The CO holds ultimate responsibility for the safety and navigation of the vessel.

Lessons Influencing Post-War Submarine Design or Tactics:

- **Robust Design for Arctic Operations:** While not solely attributable to *S-27*, the experiences in the Aleutians highlighted the need for more robust hull designs capable of operating reliably in extreme weather, rough seas, and potential ice conditions.

- **Integrated Sensor Suites:** The incident reinforced the importance of integrating all available sensors (radar, sonar, visual) into a comprehensive navigational and tactical awareness system.

- **Arctic Doctrine:** Lessons learned from the harsh realities of the Aleutian Campaign contributed to the development of specialized US Navy doctrine for operating in high latitudes, including specific navigational procedures, cold-weather survival techniques, and equipment requirements.

Relevance to Modern Submarine Operations: The core lessons from *S-27*'s loss remain highly relevant today:

- **Unwavering Navigational Vigilance:** The need for constant, accurate, and multi-sourced navigation, especially in confined waters, near coasts, or in challenging environmental conditions, is paramount.

- **Environmental Awareness:** Thorough understanding and mitigation of risks posed by weather, currents, and terrain are crucial for safe operations.

- **Command Responsibility:** The ultimate responsibility of the commanding officer for the safety and mission of the vessel, including ensuring proper watchstanding and adherence to navigational protocols, is an enduring principle of naval command.

Crew's Legacy in Naval History: The crew of the *S-27* became survivors of a lost ship in one of the war's most brutal and often-forgotten theaters. Their experience is a testament to the dangers faced by all sailors in the Aleutians, where the environment itself was often as formidable an enemy as the Japanese. The incident serves as a cautionary tale in naval history, emphasizing the critical importance of sound navigational practices, diligent watchstanding, and proactive command oversight to prevent avoidable losses, even as the larger war demanded aggressive action and calculated risks.

Glossary of Naval Terms

A

After Torpedo Room: The compartment at the stern (rear) of a submarine that houses the stern torpedo tubes, reloading equipment, and spare torpedoes.

B

Battle Surface: A command to bring the submarine to the surface rapidly to engage a target with deck guns. This maneuver minimizes the time the submarine is vulnerable while surfacing.

Bow Tubes: Torpedo tubes located in the bow (front) of the submarine.

Bridge: The open-air platform above the conning tower, used for navigation and observation by the officer of the deck and lookouts while the submarine is on the surface.

Buoyant Ascent: An emergency escape method from a sunken submarine where a survivor ascends to the surface using their natural buoyancy, without a breathing apparatus, while continuously exhaling.

C

Circular Run: A dangerous torpedo malfunction where the weapon fails to follow its set course and turns in a circle, posing a threat to the submarine that launched it.

Conning Tower: A small, pressure-tight compartment located above the submarine's main hull from which the boat is controlled. It houses periscopes, radar masts, and key attack and navigation controls.

D

Down the Throat: A high-risk torpedo attack aimed directly at the bow of an approaching enemy vessel.

E

End Around: A surface tactic, typically performed at night, where a submarine uses its superior surface speed to overtake an enemy convoy or ship, then submerges ahead of it in a favorable position for a submerged attack.

Erratic Run: A torpedo malfunction characterized by an unstable and unpredictable course, often involving porpoising or veering off course.

Escape Trunk: A small, floodable compartment (also called an escape lock) designed for crew to escape from a sunken submarine one or a few at a time.

F

Fantail: The rearmost deck area at the stern of a ship or submarine.

Fish: A common slang term for a torpedo.

Forward Torpedo Room: The compartment at the bow (front) of a submarine that houses the forward torpedo tubes, spare torpedoes, and often serves as living quarters for some of the crew.

Full Emergency Speed: The absolute maximum speed a submarine can achieve by pushing its engines or motors beyond normal operational limits, used in critical situations to attack or evade.

J

JANAC (Joint Army-Navy Assessment Committee): The official U.S. committee established during World War II to analyze and confirm claims of enemy vessels sunk or damaged by American forces.

M

Mark 18 Electric Torpedo: A U.S. Navy torpedo used in World War II powered by electric batteries. Its primary advantage was that it was wakeless, making it much more difficult for enemy ships to detect and evade compared to steam-powered torpedoes.

Momsen Lung: A breathing apparatus that allowed sailors to escape from a sunken submarine. It recycled the user's exhaled air, removing carbon dioxide and enabling them to breathe during their ascent to the surface.

P

Periscope Depth: The shallowest depth at which a submarine can travel while still being able to raise a periscope above the water's surface.

Periscope: An optical instrument consisting of tubes, lenses, and prisms that allows a submerged submarine to view the surface without fully surfacing.

Porpoising: The erratic motion of a malfunctioning torpedo as it alternately broaches the surface and dives deep, resembling the movement of a porpoise.

Presidential Unit Citation: The highest unit award presented to a U.S. military unit for extraordinary heroism in action against an armed enemy.

S

SJ Radar: A U.S. Navy surface-search radar system widely used on submarines during World War II. It enabled submarines to detect other ships and landmasses, especially at night or in poor visibility.

Spread: A firing tactic where multiple torpedoes are launched in quick succession with slightly different bearings. This increases the probability of hitting a moving or evading target.

Stern Tubes: Torpedo tubes located in the stern (rear) of the submarine.

T

Torpedo Data Computer (TDC): A complex mechanical analog computer used on U.S. submarines. It integrated data on the submarine's course and speed with the target's estimated range, bearing, and speed to calculate a firing solution for the torpedoes.

W

War Patrol: An operational deployment of a submarine into enemy-controlled waters during wartime. The primary mission was to sink enemy shipping and conduct reconnaissance.

Most Important Passages

Official Report of S-27 Grounding and Loss

In compliance with reference (a), it is reported that the U.S.S. S-27 was grounded and lost on June 19, 1942. Enclosure (A), setting forth the circumstances is forwarded herewith. Article 841(3) U.S. Navy Regulations has been complied with by an identical report forwarded direct to the Secretary of the Navy. (p. 9)

Significance: This is the official notification to the chain of command about the loss of USS S-27, establishing the date and formal reporting procedures. It represents the strategic importance of the incident requiring direct reporting to the Secretary of the Navy.

Court of Inquiry Convening at Dutch Harbor

The board met at 0915 a.m. Present: Commander Charles C. Phleger, U. S. Navy, member; Lieutenant Commander Thomas C. Thomas, U. S. Navy, member; and Lieutenant Commander Jay S. Anderson, U. S. Navy, member and acting as recorder. The recorder introduced Anthony C. Tarr, Civil Service CAF-6, as reporter. The convening order, hereto prefixed, was read and the board determined upon its procedure and decided to sit with closed doors. The board was opened. (p. 27)

Significance: Documents the formal investigation process following the submarine's loss, showing the Navy's systematic approach to determining accountability and lessons learned from the disaster.

Commander's Statement on Submarine Material Condition

Well, the only thing I have to go on there is, about two days before the last boarding, I think it was, I went aboard and the torpedo room was completely flooded. Before we had left the ship, the ballast tanks had ruptured. (p. 45)

Significance: Reveals critical mechanical failures that occurred after grounding, including flooded torpedo room and ruptured ballast tanks, which made salvage impossible and forced abandonment of the vessel.

Navigation Equipment Failures Before Grounding

A. I had made no celestial observations for several days prior because of availability of land fixes and lack of celestial objects and low visibility. A. I do not know. There is no tide data available for this vicinity. A. We noticed that high tide appeared to be roughly around midnight and low tide around noon. The rise and fall appeared to be about two feet. A. Our magnetic compass was entirely unreliable. I had no deviation tables. (p. 36)

Significance: Documents the navigation challenges faced by the submarine, including unreliable magnetic compass, lack of celestial observations, and absence of accurate tide data - all contributing factors to the grounding.

Chief of Watch Testimony on Collision Alarm

I took the watch over at twelve o'clock and we were laying to charging batteries. We secured the starboard engine at about twenty-five minutes after twelve and went ahead on course three zero five, I believe. In just a few minutes – I would say two or three minutes before three they sent down word to change course to the left at full left rudder and come to two two five and report to the captain that he thought he had sighted breakers or something. We got the word up and the captain got up and went to the bridge right away. We hit about the time along there, is about all that happened. The rest of the time I took orders from the bridge and carried them out. (p. 63)

Significance: Provides firsthand testimony of the moments leading to the grounding, showing the sudden recognition of danger and the immediate response, but insufficient time to avoid disaster.

Detailed Description of Grounding Impact and Damage

There is a submerged rock on the port beam. I do not know how large it is but it must be fairly good size because we couldn't get over it and then there is another rock that was submerged and that's the one that we must have gone in over that we couldn't get back over again. Then on the starboard side there is a rock that is about fifteen or twenty feet long. Then ahead you have got the main shore line of the island. There are large rocks dead ahead of the ship that are separated from the shore. There is a little water ahead of it before it gets to the main part of the island. (p. 45)

Significance: Provides crucial tactical information about the grounding site's geography, explaining why the submarine became trapped and could not be refloated, essential for understanding the loss.

Crew Abandonment and Survival Conditions

At 10:00 a.m. the officers and crew of the U.S.S. S-27 mustered at the submarine base barracks. The recorder read the official report of the commanding officer of the U.S.S. S-27 containing the narrative of the disaster, in the presence of the commanding officer and all the surviving officers and crew, appended hereto marked 'A'. The defendant was duly sworn. (p. 27)

Significance: Documents the formal muster of survivors and the beginning of official testimony, representing the human element of the disaster and the Navy's duty to account for all personnel.

Visibility and Weather Conditions During Watch

When I came on to relieve Mr. Butler I would estimate visibility at two miles. You could not see the horizon but it was not raining and there was possibly a fog or mist near the horizon which blotted it from view. I did not feel that the visibility decreased to such an extent as to report it to the commanding officer. I recall looking through the binoculars trying to see the horizon but I could not see it. However, I felt that possibly it was clearing up as it got darker, as the visibility seemed to me to be the same throughout the watch. (p. 72)

Significance: Critical testimony about environmental conditions that contributed to the grounding, showing how poor visibility prevented early detection of land and affected navigation decisions.

Tide and Current Analysis by Commander

Well, I have seen the tide – out there, you know, sometimes you will have two high tides and two low tides in twenty-four hours and other times you will have one high tide and one low tide in twenty-four hours. I don't think there are any regulations as far as tides out there. You take False Pass, for instance. The same thing any place where you have the heavy currents you have in these passes. I don't think you can figure the tides out. When I go out there I remember I meet up the tide for instance at Fiska, and make a note in my log book to that effect and I figure six and a half hours. If I have a high tide at noon I will have a low tide at six. In other words, on these – around, say, for instance, on the first quarter or last quarter they probably will run twelve hours one way and twelve hours the other way. On the new and full moon they will run six hours or something like that. (p. 54)

Significance: Reveals the commander's understanding of the complex and unpredictable tidal patterns in Aleutian waters, highlighting the navigational challenges unique to this theater of operations.

Final Official Loss Report to Pacific Fleet

In compliance with reference (a), it is reported that the U.S.S. S-27 was grounded and lost on June 19, 1942. Enclosure (A), setting forth the circumstances is forwarded herewith. Article 841(3) U.S. Navy Regulations has been complied with by an identical report forwarded direct to the Secretary of the Navy. (p. 81)

Significance: The final official documentation of the submarine's loss being forwarded through the command structure, representing the completion of the investigation and formal acknowledgment of the vessel's loss to the Pacific Fleet.

War Patrol Reports

START OF REEL
JOB NO. H-108
AR-195-77

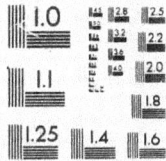

1.0
1.1
1.25 1.4 1.6
2.8 2.5
3.2 2.2
3.6 2.0
1.8

OPERATOR *R. March Jr.*

DATE *4-29-77*

THIS MICROFILM IS THE PROPERTY OF THE UNITED STATES GOVERNMENT

MICROFILMED BY
NPPSO–NAVAL DISTRICT WASHINGTON
MICROFILM SECTION

REEL TARGET, START & END
NAVEXOS 3968

S-27 (ss-132)

WWII File

All Material In This Packet Is Declassified

Dictionary of

American Naval

Fighting Ships

VOLUME VI

Historical Sketches—Letters R through S

Appendices—Submarine Chasers (SC)
Eagle-Class Patrol Craft (PE)

WITH A FOREWORD BY
ADMIRAL JAMES L. HOLLOWAY III, United States Navy,
THE CHIEF OF NAVAL OPERATIONS

AND AN INTRODUCTION BY
VICE ADMIRAL EDWIN B. HOOPER, United States Navy, Retired,
THE DIRECTOR OF NAVAL HISTORY

NAVAL HISTORY DIVISION
DEPARTMENT OF THE NAVY
WASHINGTON: 1976

Dictionary of

American Naval

Fighting Ships

VOLUME VI

Historical Sketches—Letters R through S

Appendices—Submarine Chasers (SC)
Eagle-Class Patrol Craft (PE)

WITH A FOREWORD BY
ADMIRAL JAMES L. HOLLOWAY III, United States Navy,
THE CHIEF OF NAVAL OPERATIONS

AND AN INTRODUCTION BY
VICE ADMIRAL EDWIN B. HOOPER, United States Navy, Retired,
THE DIRECTOR OF NAVAL HISTORY

NAVAL HISTORY DIVISION
DEPARTMENT OF THE NAVY
WASHINGTON: 1976

hostilities. On 11 September 1945, she sailed for San Francisco where she was decommissioned on 2 November. Fourteen days later, her name was struck from the Navy list. Her hulk was subsequently sold for scrapping and was delivered to the purchaser, Salco Iron and Metal Co., San Francisco, on 15 November 1946.

S-23 was awarded one battle star for her World War II service.

S-24

(SS–129: dp. 854 (surf.), 1,062 (subm.); l. 219'3"; b. 20'8"; dr. 15'11"; s. 14.5 k. (surf.), 11 k. (subm.); cpl. 42; a. 4 21" tt., 1 4"; cl. *S-1*)

S-24 (SS–129) was laid down on 1 November 1918 by the Bethlehem Shipbuilding Corp., Quincy, Mass.; launched on 27 June 1922; sponsored by Mrs. Herbert B. Loper; and commissioned on 24 August 1923, Lt. Comdr. Louis E. Denfeld in command.

Operating from New London, Conn., in 1923 and 1924, *S-24* served at St. Thomas, Virgin Islands, in February 1924. She visited Trinidad from 6 to 13 March, the Panama Canal area in April of that year and Hawaii from 27 April to May 1925. Next, into 1930, she served principally at San Diego, San Pedro, and Mare Island. In addition to service in the Panama Canal area in February and March 1926 and again in February 1929, *S-24* visited Hawaii in 1927 and 1928, and twice in 1929. Sailing from San Diego on 1 December 1930, she arrived at Pearl Harbor on the 12th. From then into 1938, *S-24* operated at Pearl Harbor. Departing from Pearl Harbor on 15 October, she returned to New London on 4 January 1939.

After serving with a partial crew at New London from 1 April of that year, *S-24* resumed full duty on 1 July 1940. Following duty out of New London during that year and into 1941, *S-24* served next in waters *near the Panama Canal from late December into May 1942.* Returning to New London on the 21st, *S-24* decommissioned there on 19 August 1942, and was transferred on that date to the United Kingdom, in whose navy she became HMS *P. 555.* Returned to the U.S. Navy at the end of the war in Europe, *S-24* was struck from the Navy list and was intentionally destroyed on 25 August 1947.

S-25

(SS–130: dp. 854 (surf.), 1,062 (subm.); l. 219'3"; b. 20'8"; dr. 15'11" (mean); s. 14.5 k. (surf.), 11 k. (subm.); cpl. 42; a. 1 4", 4 21" tt.; cl. *S-1*)

S-25 (SS–130) was laid down on 26 October 1918 by the Fore River Shipbuilding Corp., Quincy, Mass.; launched on 29 May 1922; sponsored by Mrs. Ross P. Schlabach; and commissioned on 9 July 1923, Lt. Comdr. George H. Fort in command.

Operating from New London, Conn., in 1923, *S-25* participated in winter maneuvers in the Caribbean and Panama Canal Zone area from January into April 1924. Then transferred to the west coast, she operated primarily in the waters off southern California into 1931. Fleet problems and division exercises during that period took her back to Panama from March into May 1927 and in February 1929 and to Hawaii in 1927, 1928, and 1930. Transferred again, she sailed from San Diego on 15 April 1931; arrived at Pearl Harbor on the 25th; and from then into 1939 operated in Hawaiian waters.

S-25 cleared Pearl Harbor to return to the Atlantic on 16 June of that year and arrived at New London on 25 August. Voyage repairs followed and in February 1940, she was assigned to a test and evaluation division there. In December, she was detached and ordered to Key West, where she provided training services into

186

May 1941, then returned to New London to prepare for transfer under the terms of the Lend Lease Agreement.

S-25 was decommissioned on 4 November 1941, and transferred, simultaneously, to Great Britain. Renamed HMS *P. 551,* she was then loaned to the government of Poland, in exile, and was accepted by Lt. Comdr. B. Romanowski of the Polish Navy and commissioned as *Jastrzab. Jastrzab* was mistakenly sunk by Allied convoy escorts off Norway on 2 May 1942.

S-26

(SS–131: dp. 854 (surf.), 1,062 (subm.); l. 219'3"; b. 20'8"; dr. 15'11"; s. 14.5 k. (surf.), 11 k. (subm.); cpl. 42; a. 4 21" tt., 1 4"; cl. *S-1*)

S-26 (SS–131) was laid down on 7 November 1919 by the Bethlehem Shipbuilding Corp., Quincy, Mass.; launched on 22 August 1922; sponsored by Mrs. Carlos Bean; and commissioned on 15 October 1923, Lt. Edmund W. Burrough in command.

Operating out of New London, Conn., from 1923 into 1926, *S-26* visited St. Thomas and Trinidad from January into April 1924, and Hawaii from 27 April to 30 May 1925. Cruising from California ports, mainly Mare Island, San Diego, and San Pedro, *S-26* visited Hawaii in the summers of 1927, 1928, 1929, and 1930. She also served in the Panama Canal area from March into May 1927, and in February 1929. Departing San Diego on 1 December 1930, she arrived at Pearl Harbor on the 12th. From then into 1938, *S-26* served at Pearl Harbor. Sailing from there on 15 October 1938, she returned to New London on 25 March 1939. Entering a period of partial duty on 15 April that year, she resumed full duty on 1 July 1940.

Following duty at New London and hydrogen tests at Washington, D.C., *S-26* sailed from New London on 10 December 1941, and arrived at Coco Solo, C.Z., on the 19th. Rammed by *PC-160* at night in the Gulf of Panama, *S-26* sank on 24 January 1942 with the loss of 46 men. Three men survived. Her hull was not salvaged.

S-27

(SS–132: dp. 854 (surf.), 1,062 (subm.); l. 219'3"; b. 20'8"; dr. 15'11" (mean); s. 14.5 k. (surf.), 11 k. (subm.); cpl. 42; a. 1 4", 4 21" tt.; cl. *S-1*)

S-27 (SS–132), authorized in March 1917, was laid down on 11 April 1919 by the Fore River Plant, Bethlehem Shipbuilding Corp., Quincy, Mass.; launched on 18 October 1922; sponsored by Mrs. Frank Baldwin; and commissioned at Groton, Conn., on 22 January 1924, Lt. Theodore Waldschmidt in command.

Based at New London through 1924, *S-27* was transferred to the Pacific in 1925; and, after exercises in the Hawaiian Islands during the spring of that year, she arrived at her new homeport, San Diego, in June. She remained based in southern California through the decade and, except for fleet maneuvers, operated primarily off that coast. Fleet maneuver exercises, and problems took her to the west coast of Central America; to the Panama Canal Zone; into the Caribbean; and to Hawaii. In 1931, she was transferred to Hawaii; and, on 23 February, she arrived at Pearl Harbor, whence she operated until mid-1939. On 16 June 1939, she sailed east; and, on the 27th, she arrived at San Diego and resumed operations off the southern California coast.

For the next two and a half years, she conducted exercises and tests off that coast, primarily for the Underwater Sound Training School. In late November 1941, she proceeded to Mare Island, where she was undergoing overhaul when the United States entered World War II.

On 23 January 1942, *S-27* stood out of San Francisco Bay and moved south. Three days later, she returned to San Diego and resumed operations for the Sound School which she continued into the spring. Then ordered north, to the Aleutians, she departed San Diego on 20 May; steamed to Port Angeles; thence, continued on to Alaskan waters where she commenced patrol operations in June. On the 12th, a little over a week after the beginning of the war in the Aleutians, she put into Dutch Harbor, took on provisions, refueled, and then headed west with orders to patrol in the Kuluk Bay area and to reconnoiter Constantine Harbor, Amchitka. On the night of 16–17 June, she was ordered to Kiska. On the 18th, she reconnoitered Constantine Harbor; found no signs of enemy activity in that evacuated village; and moved on to round the southern end of the island, whence she would proceed to Kiska. In mid-afternoon, she rounded East Cape and that night when she surfaced, fog obscured her position. Lying to to charge on both engines, she was carried about five miles from her estimated (DR) position. The fog prevented knowledge of the drift. At midnight she got underway, slowly, on one engine and continued to charge on the other. Soon after 0043 on the 19th, breakers were sighted about 25 yards forward of the bow. "Back emergency" orders were given. Seconds later, she grounded on rocks off St. Makarius Point.

Waves bumped her violently against the rocks, rolling her 10 to 15 degrees on each side. Her motors were continued at "back emergency," but she was held firm by a submerged rock. Fuel was blown. Efforts to back off were continued, but the lightened ship swung harder against the rocks. Her starboard screw struck a rock and was disabled.

Efforts were made to force the ship ahead to clear the stern; but, she could move only about twenty feet forward before she was again held fast. The immediate area was sounded. No passage was found. The seas continued to pound her.

By 0330, the pounding had increased and plans were made to move the greater part of the crew off. Dispatches of her plight, sent first at 0115, were continued. Six were sent in all. One, giving no position, was received at Dutch Harbor.

A ferry system, using a rubber boat and lines rigged between the ship and the beach, was set up. Men, provisions, clothing, guns, and medical supplies were transferred safely. By 1100, all but six, the commanding officer, Lt. H. L. Jukes, and five others, were ashore. All equipment was destroyed. Classified material was burned. At 1530, three of the remaining men went ashore. The side plating was now loose; the torpedo room was flooding. At 1550, the radioman, executive officer, and commanding officer left the submarine.

The night of 19–20 June was spent in an unsheltered cove. On the 20th, camp was set up at Constantine Harbor, using the buildings and heating equipment which had survived a Japanese bombing. By the 21st, the camp was fully organized; routines, including sentries and lookouts, had been established. Trips to and from the cove continued for three days. *S-27* was reboarded on the 21st and 22d; thereafter, the presence of chlorine gas prohibited further visits to take off more supplies.

On the 24th, a PBY on a routine flight spotted the activity at Constantine Harbor; landed; and took off 15 of the survivors. On the 25th, three planes were sent in to bring off the remainder. All guns salvaged from *S-27* were destroyed. Nothing was left except the submarine's hulk and canned provisions, blankets, and winter clothing.

S-28

(SS-133: dp. 854 (surf.), 1,062 (subm.); l. 219'3"; b. 20'8"; dr. 15'11" (mean); s. 14.5 k. (surf.), 11 k. (subm.); cpl. 42; a. 1 4", 4 21" tt.; cl. *S-1*)

S-28 (SS-133) was laid down on 16 April 1919 by the Bethlehem Shipbuilding Corp., Quincy, Mass.; launched on 20 September 1922; sponsored by Mrs. William R. Monroe; and commissioned on 13 December 1923, Lt. Kemp C. Christian in command.

Following shakedown exercises off the southern New England coast, *S-28* moved south in March 1924 to join Submarine Division (SubDiv) 11. In the final exercises of that year's winter maneuvers in the Caribbean. In April, she returned to New London with her division and commenced local exercises which occupied the remainder of the year. With the winter of 1925, she moved south again; transited the Panama Canal; and, after the conclusion of Fleet Problem V—conducted in the vicinity of Guadalupe Island—she arrived in the Hawaiian Islands for a month's stay. In June, she moved east, to San Diego, where her division replaced another which had been transferred to the Asiatic Fleet.

Into 1931, the submarine operated primarily off southern California deploying for fleet problems in the Panama Canal area in 1926 and 1929; for summer maneuvers in Hawaiian waters in 1927 and 1930; and for regularly scheduled overhaul periods at Mare Island Navy Yard throughout the period.

She departed the west coast for Hawaii in mid-February 1931 and, on the 23d, arrived at Pearl Harbor, whence she operated for the next eight and one-half years. In mid-1939, she was transferred back to San Diego, where she was based until after the United States entered World War II.

On 7 December 1941, *S-28*, then a unit of SubDiv 41, was undergoing overhaul at Mare Island. On 22 January 1942, the work was completed, and she returned to San Diego, where she resumed her prewar training activities for the Underwater Sound Training School. She continued that duty into the spring; then was ordered north, to the Aleutians, to augment the defenses of that Alaskan island chain which rimmed the north Pacific.

On 20 May, *S-28*, with other submarines of her division, departed San Diego. Five days later, they topped off at Port Angeles, then continued on toward the newly established submarine base at Dutch Harbor, Unalaska. On the 29th, however, as preparations were made to minimize a two-pronged Japanese thrust against Midway and the Aleutians, the S-boats were directed to proceed to their stations, bypassing Dutch Harbor.

During a quickly extinguished fire in her port main motor on the morning of 1 June, *S-28* suffered minor damage. That evening, she parted company with her sister ships and their escort; and, the next day, she entered her assigned area and commenced patrolling the approaches to Cold Bay on the tip of the Alaskan Peninsula. On the 3d, the Japanese bombed Dutch Harbor to open the war in the Aleutians; and, within the week, they had occupied Kiska and Attu. On the 12th, *S-28* arrived at Dutch Harbor; refueled; took on provisions; and headed west to resume her war patrol. On the 15th, she crossed the 180th meridian; and, on the 17th, after a two-day storm, she sighted Kiska and set a course to intercept enemy shipping between there and Attu. On the 18th, she fired on her first enemy target, a destroyer, and was in turn attacked. Eight hours later, sounds of the destroyer's search faded out to the south. *S-28* had survived her first encounter with Japanese antisubmarine warfare tactics.

Poor weather soon returned and storms raged during eighty percent of her remaining time on station. On the 28th, she moored in Dutch Harbor and commenced refit. On 15 July, she got underway and again headed

187

UNITED STATES
SUBMARINE LOSSES

WORLD WAR II

Reissued with an Appendix of
Axis Submarine Losses, fully indexed,

by

Naval History Division
Office of the Chief of Naval Operations
Washington: 1963

S-27 (SS 132)

In June of 1942, the enemy landed on Kiska Island in the Aleutians and the U. S. Fleet was interested in Amchitka Island, 60 miles east of Kiska. S-27, on her first patrol, with Lt. H. L. Jukes in command, was sent to make a reconnaissance of Constantine Harbor, at Amchitka, and then to go around the island and patrol off Kiska. By 19 June 1942, the reconnaissance was completed, and S-27 started for her area.

In the Aleutian area at that time of year there is daylight eighteen hours of the twenty-four, and when S-27 surfaced at 2200 on the night of 19 June, after the necessarily prolonged submergence during daylight hours, her batteries were badly in need of charging. Navigating only by DR since she had no radar or fathometer, S-27 gained a position well off the land, and hove to in order to charge batteries. While she was lying to, currents took her about five miles from her DR position, although fog prevented knowledge of it at the time. At about 2240 on 19 June, S-27 was able to go ahead on one engine while charging on the other. Almost immediately, she struck a reef about 400 yards from Amchitka Island and rolled over into a rocky basin.

All efforts to get off the rocks were futile, and of six dispatches sent telling her plight, only one, which did not give her position, was picked up. The torpedo room was flooding, the after battery was getting wet and generating chlorine, and the boat had an eight to twelve-degree down angle. The ship was abandoned, and all hands were taken ashore in a rubber lifeboat. They spent the night huddled around fires, and the next morning set out for the village at Constantine Harbor, across the island. There they found a church and two buildings, the Japanese having bombed the rest, but no inhabitants. Food, guns, and ammunition had been salvaged from the ship and the men were organized by the Commanding Officer into a regular military camp.

H. L. Jukes

On the sixth day a PBY flew over, sighted the men and landed. He took 12 men and an officer back to Dutch Harbor and the next morning three other PBY's flew out for the rest of the men. The crew survived this disaster without a single injury or case of illness.

26

10

SS132/L11-1/A4-1   U.S.S. S-27

Serial (031)   June 29, 1942.

~~DECLASSIFIED~~ A L

From: The Commanding Officer.
To :   The Commander-in-Chief, U.S. Fleet.
Via :   (1) The Commander Submarine Division
                Forty One.
            (2) The Commander Submarine Squadron Four.
            (3) The Commander Submarines, Pacific Fleet.
            (4) The Commander-in-Chief, Pacific Fleet.

Subject: U.S.S. S-27 (SS132) - Grounding and Subsequent
            Loss of.

Reference: (a) Article 840 U.S. Navy Regulations.

Enclosure: (A) Narrative of events prior to the grounding
                and subsequent loss of the U.S.S. S-27 and
                the events immediately afterwards.

     1.   In compliance with reference (a), it is reported
that the U.S.S. S-27 was grounded and lost on June 19, 1942.

     2.   Enclosure (A), setting forth the circumstances
is forwarded herewith.

     3.   Article 841(3) U.S. Navy Regulations has been
complied with by an identical report forwarded direct to the
Secretary of the Navy.

                              H. L. JUKES

ENCLOSURE "A"

The following is a narrative of the events prior to the grounding and subsequent loss of the U.S.S. S-27 and the events immediately afterwards.

After surfacing on the night of 16 June 1942, we received a message directing us to leave our patrol area off of KULUK BAY and proceed to assigned area at KISKA ISLAND via AMCHITKA PASS. Prior to leaving DUTCH HARBOR for patrol I had received verbal orders from the Division Commander to inspect CONSTANTINE HARBOR, AMCHITKA ISLAND for the presence of enemy activity.

The course was set to clear to the northward of the islands by five miles and the distance to travel indicated our arrival off CONSTANTINE HARBOR about 0100 (plus 12) on the 18th. of June. We were able to obtain fixes until we rounded GARELOI ISLAND and headed across AMCHITKA PASS on course 245°T. At 2345 I went to the bridge to see if AMCHITKA ISLAND had been sighted and to be present if a landfall was made. At 2400 when nothing could be seen ahead I changed course to 270°T. in order to make certain of landfall in case the current, (of which I had no information) had set us to the south and east during the passage. After steaming for one hour at two thirds speed (8 knots) on this course 270°T. without sighting anything the decision was made to circle with 10° rudder until light conditions were better. I was concerned about being able to see land because the Coast Pilot and the Confidential Chart showed that the entire island was low and we might not have been able to see it in time to prevent grounding. This was done even knowing that the 0100 D.R. position still gave me 7½ miles of open water.

At 0204 steadied on course 090°T. and dived at 0207. From that time until 0556 we steered various courses until I picked up the island and obtained a fix. There after we patrolled until 1200 when I decided that I should leave if I wanted to get around the southern end before time to surface and charge batteries. It was deemed advisable to stay submerged during daylight because the enemy was known to be within 70 miles and I had no report of their air activities.

The decision to round the island to the southward was based upon the following factors:

1. Previous reports received indicated the presence of the enemy on SEMISOPOCHNOI ISLAND. Therefore, knowing they were at KISKA ISLAND, it seemed likely that there might be air patrols between the two. A northern route for me might disclose my presence and I wanted to reach my area (090°T. to 120°T. from north head KISKA HARBOR) undetected if possible.

- 1 -

ENCLOSURE "A"

2. To have entered my area from the north would have hemmed me in by RAT ISLAND, LITTLE SITKIN ISLAND and subsequently the unknown currents of OGLALA PASS and RAT ISLAND PASS where little enemy surface shipping might be expected, whereas a southern approach left me free water to the south for movement and retirement if necessary.

3. I had decided to run my patrol on a northwest - southeast line five to ten miles southwest of RAT ISLAND and TANADAK PASS retiring at night to the south, or southeast to charge batteries. Consequently, the southern approach, rounding AMCHITKA to the south, seemed to me the most logical route.

After rounding EAST CAPE on AMCHITKA ISLAND at 1330 numerous tangential fixes were obtained and a set to the north of about two knots was determined. Currents of this magnitude are known to exist and had been previously encountered in other ALEUTIAN ISLAND PASSES. Consequently, at 1735 speed was increased to 6 knots and course adjusted in order to permit rounding ST MAKARIUS PT. and being at least five miles from the island prior to 2000 when it would be necessary to surface and lie to for a charge for a period of at least four hours. I felt that this position would remove me from the influence of the currents in the PASS. No information on currents to be encountered in any part of my area was available.

At 1920 the ship was surfaced, visibility from 2 - 3 miles, and the island was not in sight because of a fog bank.

In order to close the line which I had decided to steer for my area I went ahead at 1929 on course 315°T. at a speed of 6 knots and stopped at 2005 in order to start the battery charge. The D.R. position at this time placed the ship 6 miles west of ST MAKARIUS PT. It had been my policy to lie to and charge about 5-6 miles off of any land available. I felt that this position provided the least chance of detection either by RADAR or VISUAL search because of our blending with the shore background.

At 2010 the charge was started and at 2015 I was relieved of the deck by the O.O.D. Conditions at this time were: Visibility 2-3 miles, calm sea, sky overcast and the island not in sight. I instructed the O.O.D. and lookouts to be especially on the alert for land.

At 2030 the oncoming O.O.D. for the 2100 to 0000 watch was given the same instructions by me as to alertness for land.

At 2200 the night order book was written and made available for the O.O.D. In the night order book instructions were given to set course 305°T. speed 6 knots when one engine was

- 2 -

ENCLOSURE "A"

released from charging, to keep a careful watch for land, and if in doubt as to position as regards proximity to beach to change course to 225°T. and to call me.

At 0027 the O.O.D. went ahead six knots on starboard engine and came left from 050°T. (upon which head the vessel lay to) to 305°T. as per instructions, and informed me. At about 0043 the O.O.D. reported he was coming left to 225°T. with full left rudder as he thought he had sighted land on the starboard bow. I immediately started for the bridge and simultaneously the ship struck.

The sequence of events that immediately preceded the grounding, as reported by the O.O.D. Boatswain T. E. Krueger, U.S. Navy, are as follows:

"A dark object believed to be land, suddenly loomed up about one point on the starboard bow and was sighted simultaneously by the O.O.D., quartermaster and starboard lookout. The O.O.D. ordered "left full rudder, come to course 225°T. and report to the captain that I think I have sighted land on the starboard bow and am changing course to 225°T." Almost immediately thereafter the O.O.D. saw small breakers about 25 yards forward of the bow and rang up "back emergency", on both engine order telegraphs and sounded the collision alarm. The ship struck almost immediately thereafter."

I arrived on the bridge at this time. The port motor was backing and the starboard started backing within a few seconds and the ship was reported rigged for collision. The ship was bumping violently on the rocks and rolling about 10° to 15° on each side. The motors were continued at back emergency until it was seen that the vessel was held from going astern by a submerged rock. Orders were then given to blow the fuel from No. 3 Main Ballast Tank, the after fuel group and all variable tanks. Efforts were continued to back clear as the vessel became lighter during which time a tendency for the stern to swing to starboard against rocks was established, and the starboard screw struck and was disabled. It was necessary to force the ship ahead in order to clear the stern. During this period it was found that the ship could be moved only about 20 feet forward or aft before it became held fast. Attempts were continued until all tanks were blown dry with the exception of a small amount of fuel amidships.

After these attempts to clear by backing and filling had failed the area was sounded for possible passage through which the vessel might be warped but none was found.

At 0115 the first message was encoded and broadcast. In all, five were sent. They appear at the end of this narrative.

- 3 -

ENCLOSURE "A"

At 0330 plans were made to remove the greater part of the crew because the pounding was increasing and I felt that the tanks might give at any moment resulting in danger to the crew that could be avoided. The rubber life boat was brought up on deck and made ready. One officer and one man, both capable swimmers, were first sent in to the beach and reported back that conditions were favorable once the boat cleared the first rocks close to the ship. A "ferry" system was then used with lines to the boat and the beach. Provisions, dry and warm clothing, guns, medical supplies and men were safely transferred. By about 1100 all but five men and myself were landed. By this time the breakers had increased so that further trips for provisions were not safe.

Prior to leaving the ship the following equipment which I considered might prove advantageous to the enemy if discovered was completely destroyed:

1. ECM:- all wheels broken and scattered in deep water. Typewriter part destroyed by hammer and thrown in deep water. Nothing remains in ship but the safe which is empty.

2. QC - JK equipment demolished with hammer. QC head was run out when vessel grounded.

3. JK in torpedo room demolished.

4. Mk 8 Torpedo Angle solver thrown overboard as far as possible seaward.

5. All torpedo approach data and tables burned.

6. All confidential and secret publications, codes, ciphers and crypto aids were taken ashore and burned. Unburnable confidential items were broken and thrown in deep water.

At 1530 three of the remaining men were gotten ashore. At this time the heavy pounding had definitely loosened the side plating for it could be heard rattling at each jar of the ship. The torpedo room was slowly flooding although an air pressure had been built up in this compartment. An angle of six degrees down by the head was noticed. The propellers were clear of the water.

At 1550 as nothing could be done further to help the ship, and the torpedo room was about one half flooded, I decided to leave. The remaining compartments were made watertight and the radioman, second officer and myself went ashore.

Crew and provisions had been landed in an unsheltered cove, the surface of which was covered with rocks and small boulders.

- 4 -

ENCLOSURE "A"

Fires had been started and wet clothing removed. No injuries
were reported and aside from being exhausted the crew was in very
good condition. Each man was given about 1½ ounces of pure
alcohol in hot coffee. Fires were going all night but because
of the very cold wind and rain no rest was obtained.

At 0430 on the 20th. of June all hands except 10 started
out to search for Constantine Harbor. The inspection by periscope on the previous day disclosed a church and a few small
buildings there. By 0900 all had arrived at the deserted village.
The buildings proved adequate for the entire crew. Coal, diesel
oil and gasoline were available and stoves rigged in three buildings.

On the following day camp routine was established, fourteen
camp orders published, armed sentries and lookouts were posted
and a regular routine was put into effect. This was done in order
to provide something for the men to do and to prevent any attempts
at slackness in discipline. The entire crew responded admirably
throughout this entire period and it was noted that each man tried
to pull even more than his own weight.

The next three days were spent in trips to the cove for
supplies. The ship was boarded on the 21st. and 22nd. by me and
a volunteer party, and more provisions landed. Trips to the ship
were only possible during early morning. Conditions aboard were
becoming worse. On the 21st. I boarded and found the forward
battery compartment begining to flood. Chlorine gas was present
so no further attempts were made to enter this compartment. The
control room bilges were about 2/3 filled. Other compartments
dry. Landing on board was becoming difficult due to the increased
down angle which allowed the seas to break over the only place
available to land. On the last trip the hatches were closed and
no further trips were attempted.

Provisions obtained could last for about 30 days by rationing. This was started on the first day ashore for I had no knowledge as to whether my last two messages had been received and I
also felt that our nearness to the enemy might prevent rescue
until some late date.

On 24 June a PBY plane circled and landed. The pilot had
been on a routine flight and fortunately passed over the Harbor.
Fifteen of the crew were rescued. On 25 June three planes removed
the remainder of the crew.

All guns salvaged from the ship were destroyed. Nothing
of value remains at Constantine Harbor except canned provisions,
blankets and winter clothing.

H. L. JUKES

APPENDIX TO NARRATIVE

COPIES OF MESSAGES SENT AND RECEIVED ON 19 JUNE 1942, CONTD.

MESSAGES RECEIVED

1. WHAT IS YOUR POSITION X USE SECRET CRYPTO CHANNEL X
AMPLIFY REPORT OF SCREWS DISABLED.

    FROM: CTG 8.5
    TIME: 0530 (plus 12)

2. MY NINETEEN SEVENTEEN THIRTY REQUESTED POSITION AND DETAILS
SAIL TWENTY SEVEN X ESTIMATED POSITION VICINITY AMCHITKA
ISLAND.

    FROM: CSD41
    TO : COMALSEC
    INFO: S-27
    TIME: 0754 (plus 12)

3. WHAT IS YOUR POSITION ANSWER SECURE CYPHER IF NOT IN TROUBLE.

    FROM: ANY OR ALL U.S. SHIPS
    TO : S-27
    TIME: 0849 (plus 12)

APPENDIX TO NARRATIVE

COPIES OF MESSAGES SENT AND RECEIVED ON 19 JUNE 1942.

MESSAGES SENT

1. AGROUND POUNDING SOUTHEAST SIDE AMCHITKA ISLAND.

    TIME - 0115 (plus 12)
    ADDRESSED TO ANY OR ALL U.S. SHIPS.
    FREQUENCIES USED: 8270, 12705, 4305.
    AIRCRAFT CODE USED.

2. TUG CAN GET US OFF SCREWS DISABLED.

    TIME - 0145.
    ADDRESSED TO - ANY OR ALL U.S. NAVY SHIPS.
    FREQUENCIES: - 8270, 12705, 4305, 8190.
    AIRCRAFT CODE USED.

3. IMPROPERLY CODED.

    SENT AT 0440 (plus 12)

4. CANCEL MY NINETEEN SIXTEEN FORTY X WEDGED SOLIDLY ST.
    MAKARIUS REPEAT ST. MAKARIUS POINT AMCHITKA X PORT
    SCREW WORKING ON MOTOR BUT MOTOR ROOM EXPECTED TO FLOOD
    ANY TIME X UNABLE TO BACK OVER ROCKS X BELIEVE CAN BE
    PULLED CLEAR BY TUG X ALL TANKS DRY X POUNDING IS BAD X
    AM PREPARED TO ABANDON X HEAVY FOG.

    SENT TO CSD41, INFO CTF 8.
    FREQUENCIES USED: 8270, 12705, 4305, CSP 1037(A) AND
    1038(A) USED.

5. HEAVY POUNDING CONTINUES X HELPLESS X SEAMS GONE IN
    BALLAST TANKS X ALL ASHORE EXCEPT SIX X ALL COMPARTMENT DRY
    BUT TORPEDO ROOM X WILL STAY UNTIL UNTENABLE X CRYPTO
AIDS DESTROYED BUT THIS X WHEN ABANDONED WILL TAKE CREW TO
    CONSTANTINE HARBOR THIS FREE OF ENEMY ON EIGHTEENTH.

    SENT TO CSD41, CTF8, INFO. COMALSEC. CSP 1037(A) USED.
    FREQUENCY: 8270, TIME 1345 (plus 12)

6. DUE SEA CONDITIONS AM ABANDONING SHIP X IF POSSIBLE WILL
    RETURN TOMORROW OTHERWISE CONSTANTINE LY TWENTY ZERO ONE
    FORTY FIVE.

    TO CSD41, CTF8, INFO. COMALSEC.
    TIME: 1513 (plus 12)
    FREQ. 8270
    CODE: CSP 1037(A) 1038(A).

- 1 -

L11-1

```
FB41/L11-1/A4-1
Serial 1004
First Endorsement to          Submarine Division 41,
CO USS S-27 Serial            July 6, 1942.
(031) of 6/29/42
```

CONFIDENTIAL

```
From:     The Commander Submarine Division FORTY-ONE.
To  :     The Commander-in-Chief, U.S. FLEET.
Via :     (1) The Commander Task Force EIGHT.
          (2) The Commander Submarine Squadron FOUR.
          (3) The Commander Submarines, PACIFIC FLEET.
          (4) The Commander-in-Chief, U.S. PACIFIC FLEET.
```

Subject: U.S.S. S-27 (SS132) - Grounding and Subsequent
              Loss of.

1.   Forwarded.

2.   A Board of Investigation convened by order of
the Commander, Task Force EIGHT, has been directed to investi-
gate the grounding and loss of S-27.

B. G. LAKE.

Copy to: S-27

T-128

794   105

COMMANDER TASK FORCE EIGHT

L11-1

Serial T-035   July 10, 1942.

CONFIDENTIAL

SECOND ENDORSEMENT to
CO USS S-27 Serial
(031) of 6/29/42

From: Commander Task Force EIGHT.
To :   The Commander-in-Chief, U.S. Fleet.
Via : (1) Commander Submarine Squadron FOUR.
    (2) Commander Submarines, Pacific Fleet.
    (3) Commander-in-Chief, U.S. Pacific Fleet.

Subject: U.S.S. S-27 (SS132) - Grounding and Subsequent
    Loss of.

  1. Forwarded.

         R. A. Theobald
         R. A. THEOBALD.

THIRD ENDORSEMENT - - - - - SUBMARINE SQUADRON FOUR - - 70-Rh
FC5-4/L11-1

Serial 1244

CONFIDENTIAL

From: The Commander Submarine Squadron FOUR.
To :   The Commander-in-Chief, U.S. Fleet.
Via : (1) The Commander Submarines, Pacific Fleet.
    (2) The Commander-in-Chief, U.S. Pacific Fleet.

  1. Forwarded.

         J. H. Brown
         J. H. BROWN, Jr.

REFER TO NO.

FF12-10/L11-1   <u>UNITED STATES PACIFIC FLEET</u>   Sal.
Serial 0927   <u>SUBMARINES, PACIFIC FLEET</u>

CONFIDENTIAL   Care of Fleet Post Office,
                                      San Francisco, California.
                                         15 AUG 1942

FOURTH ENDORSEMENT to
CO USS S-27 Conf. ltr.
SS132/L11-1/A4-1, ser.
(031) of June 29, 1942.

From: The Commander Submarines, Pacific Fleet.
To :   The Commander-in-Chief, U.S. Fleet.
Via :   The Commander-in-Chief, U.S. Pacific Fleet.

Subject: U.S.S. S-27 (SS132) - Grounding and Subsequent
          Loss of.

    1.   Forwarded, contents noted. A copy of a Board
of Investigation in this case has been received.

                              R. H. ENGLISH.

Cincpac File No.
L11-1/C&G/(05)

Serial

UNITED STATES PACIFIC FLEET
FLAGSHIP OF THE COMMANDER-IN-CHIEF

paw

COMMANDER IN CHIEF
U. S. FLEET

CONFIDENTIAL

5th Endorsement on
CO USS S-27 Conf.
SS132/L11-1/A4-1,
Serial 031 dated
June 29, 1942.

From: Commander in Chief, U. S. Pacific Fleet.
To: Commander in Chief, U. S. Fleet.

Subject: U.S.S. S-27 (SS132) - Grounding and
         subsequent loss of.

1.   Forwarded.

2.   At the request of the Judge Advocate, U.S.S.
BLACK HAWK, the record of proceedings of the board of in-
vestigation in this case has been forwarded to the Naval
Air Station Kodiak for use in connection with the trial of
Lieutenant Commander Herbert L. Jukes, U.S. Navy, Commanding
Officer of the U.S.S. S-27, by general court-martial.

P. V. Mercer

P. V. MERCER
By direction.

Cincpac File No.
A17-25/(05)
Serial

UNITED STATES PACIFIC FLEET
Flagship of the Commander in Chief

c/o Fleet Post Office,
San Francisco, California,

DECLASSIFIED

AUG 20 1942

The proceedings, finding of facts, and opinion of the
board of investigation in the attached case, and the action
of the convening authority thereon, are approved.

C. W. NIMITZ,
Admiral, U.S. Navy,
Commander in Chief,
United States Pacific Fleet.

To: Judge Advocate General.

Copy to: Convening Authority.
             Commander Submarines, Pacific Fleet.
             Commander Submarine Division FORTY-ONE.

Cincpac File No.

A17-25/(09)

UNITED STATES PACIFIC FLEET
FLAGSHIP OF THE COMMANDER-IN-CHIEF

mc

MEMORANDUM FOR FLAG SECRETARY

Subject: Board of Investigation Convened at the U.S. Naval
Air Station, Dutch Harbor, Alaska by order of
the Commander of a Task Force, U.S. Pacific Fleet
to Inquire into and Report Upon the Grounding of
the U.S.S. S-27 that occurred on or about June
19, 1942.

1.   The following is a summary of the record in the
above entitled investigation.

Finding of Facts

The S-27 grounded on the Southeast coast of
Amchitka Island, Aleutian Islands, in approximately
latitude 51° 22' North and longitude 179° 36' 30"
east at 0043 June 19, 1942 in an authorized patrol
area. She had been lying to in order to charge
batteries and drifted into dangerous waters as
a result of unpredictable currents. Although
visibility was limited, the ship had started on
its assigned course at a speed of six knots after
charging was partially completed. Neither the
Commanding Officer nor the Navigator were on the
bridge at the time of the accident nor at any
time after the initial charging was completed.
The Officer of the Deck did not call the Captain
when visibility became worse. There was no loss
of life nor injury to personnel and no material
or equipage of any consequence was salvaged.
The provisions of sections 724 and 725 of Naval
Courts and Boards have been met.

Opinion

The tidal currents in the area of grounding are
impossible of exact determination. Salvage
operations are not practicable because of weather,
enemy and equipment. The Commanding Officer was
responsible for the grounding because a dangerous
course was set without due consideration to the
currents. The Navigator was responsible in that
he did not use all available means to fix the
position of the ship and did not advise the
Commanding Officer of the danger. The Officer of

-1-

Cinepac File No.
A17-25/(09)

UNITED STATES PACIFIC FLEET
FLAGSHIP OF THE COMMANDER-IN-CHIEF

mc

MEMORANDUM FOR FLAG SECRETARY (CONT'D)

Subject: Board of Investigation Convened at the U.S. Naval
        Air Station, Dutch Harbor, Alaska by order of
        the Commander of a Task Force, U.S. Pacific Fleet
        to inquire into and Report upon the Grounding of
        the U.S.S. S-27 that occurred on or about June
        19, 1942.

- -

the Deck was responsible to a lesser degree in that
he followed a prescribed course under bad visibility
without informing the Captain.

Action of Convening Authority

The Commanding Officer, Lieutenant Commander JUKES,
U.S. Navy ordered to be tried by a general court
martial for "through negligence suffering a vessel
of the Navy to be stranded". The Navigator, Lieuten-
ant Frank M. Smith ordered to be tried by a general
court martial for "Culpable Inefficiency in the
Performance of Duty". A letter of admonition is to be
addressed to Boatswain T.E. KRUEGER, U.S. Navy.

2.   It appears that the record of proceedings satisfies the
requirements of Naval Courts and Boards.

3.   It is recommended that the following endorsement be
attached to the record.

"The proceedings, finding of facts, and opinion of
the investigation in the attached case, and the
action of the convening authority thereon, are
approved."

Approved. Prepare smooth draft.

P.YMM.

Respectfully,

Geraghty

T. F. GERAGHTY,
Ensign D-V(S), USNR.

CONFIDENTIAL

RECORD OF PROCEEDINGS

of a

BOARD OF INVESTIGATION

Convened at the

U. S. Naval Air Station, Dutch Harbor,
Alaska,

By order of

Commander of a Task Force,
U.S. Pacific Fleet.

To inquire into and report upon the grounding of
the U.S.S. S-27 that occurred on or about June 19, 1942.

July 1, 1942

Board of investigation to inquire into and report upon the grounding of
the U.S.S. S-27 that occurred on or about June 19, 1942.

INDEX

FIRST DAY

U. S. Naval Air Station,
Dutch Harbor, Alaska.
Wednesday, July 1, 1942.

The board met at 9:15 a.m.

Present: Commander Charles C. Phleger, U. S. Navy, member;
Lieutenant Commander Thomas C. Thomas, U. S. Navy, member; and
Lieutenant Commander Jay S. Anderson, U. S. Navy, member and
acting as recorder.

The recorder introduced Anthony C. Tarr, Civil Service CAF-6, as reporter.

The convening order, hereto prefixed, was read and the board determined upon
its procedure and decided to sit with closed doors.

The board was opened.

Lieutenant Commander Herbert L. Jukes, U. S. Navy, commanding U.S.S. S-27,
entered as defendant and, with the permission of the board, introduced
Lieutenant Commander J. D. Crowley, U. S. Navy, as his counsel.

The recorder read the convening order.

The defendant was informed of his rights. The defendant stated that he did
not object to any member.

Each member and the reporter were duly sworn.

No witnesses not otherwise connected with the investigation were present.

The board adjourned at 9:45 a.m. to the submarine base barracks for the purpose of reading the commanding officer's official report to the officers and
crew of the U.S.S. S-27.

At 10:00 a.m. the officers and crew of the U.S.S. S-27 mustered at the submarine base barracks.

The recorder read the official report of the commanding officer of the U.S.S.
S-27 containing the narrative of the disaster, in the presence of the command-
ing officer and all the surviving officers and crew, appended hereto marked
"A".

The defendant was duly sworn.

Questioned by the board:

1. Q. Lieutenant Commander Herbert L. Jukes, is the narrative just read a
true statement of the loss of the S-27?

A. It is.

2. Q. Have you any complaint to make against any of the surviving officers
and crew of the said ship on that occasion?

A. I have not.   - 1 -

All the surviving officers and crew as listed below were duly sworn:

OFFICERS

F. M. Smith, Lieutenant, U. S. Navy.
O. M. Butler, Lieutenant, U. S. Navy.
L. H. Young, Lieutenant, junior grade, U. S. Naval Reserve.
T. E. Krueger, Boatswain, U. S. Navy.

CREW

Robert J. Allan, MoMM2c, U. S. Navy.
Charlie A. Bowker, MoMM1c, U. S. Navy.
Marvin E. Breedlove, CCStd(AA), U. S. Navy.
Arvil E. Carter, Y2c, U. S. Navy.
Donald E. Catron, F3c, U. S. Navy.
Edgar A. Chase, RM2c, U. S. Navy.
George D. Dinsmore, Jr., SC3c, U. S. Navy.
Douglas A. Eaker, RM1c, U. S. Navy.
James H. Ealey, Sea1c, U. S. Navy.
Frederick D. Fitzpatrick, Sea1c, U. S. Naval Reserve.
John T. Fowler, TM1c, U. S. Navy.
Glenn R. Fritch, Sea1c, U. S. Naval Reserve.
George J. Grdina, F3c, U. S. Navy.
John H. Guernsey, Sea1c, U. S. Navy.
Alonzo Henderson, F1c, U. S. Navy.
George J. Herold, Sea1c, U. S. Navy.
Scott E. Morton, Jr., Sea1c, U. S. Navy.
Victor O. Moule, RM2c, U. S. Navy.
Paul E. Huffman, CMoMM(AA), U. S. Navy.
Marvin L. Ivy, CTM(PA), U. S. Navy.
Roger A. Jernigan, F2c, U. S. Navy.
Stanley I. Jorgesen, Sea1c, U. S. Navy.
Arthur D. Kesner, CEM(PA), U. S. Navy.
Michael M. Kost, F2c, U. S. Naval Reserve.
Karl W. Kunz, MoMM1c, U. S. Navy.
Dick D. Lister, SM1c, U. S. Navy.
Russell L. Lokey, CMoMM(AA), U. S. Navy.
Earl W. Mayer, SC3c, U. S. Navy.
Harry W. McKinnon, TM2c, U. S. Navy.
Robert H. Mills, F1c, U. S. Navy.
Percy Moore, Jr., Sea1c, U. S. Navy.
John W. Myers, CMoMM(AA), U. S. Navy.
Roe D. Nelson, F2c, U. S. Navy.
Francis P. Noone, F1c, U. S. Navy.
Rocco A. Pia, GM3c, U. S. Navy.
Jesus S. Reyes, Matt1c, U. S. Navy.
Raymond G. Pugsley, MoMM2c, U. S. Navy.
Charles N. Rodina, RM3c, U. S. Navy.
Doroteo G. San Agustin, OC3c, U. S. Navy.
Robert A. Shirah, Sea1c, U. S. Navy.
Frank N. Stoltz, RM1c, U. S. Navy.
Glen A. Thurnau, F2c, U. S. Navy.
Ladislaus Topor, MoMM1c, U. S. Navy.
Leo W. Whiticar, RM3c, U. S. Navy.
Charles O. Wolber, GM1c, U. S. Navy.

Examined by the board:

1. Q. Have you any objections to make in regard to the narrative just read to the board or anything to lay to the charge of any officer or man with regard to the loss of the U.S.S. S-27?

A. No.

-2-

The board adjourned at 10:30 a.m.

The board reassembled at 10:50 a.m. at the U. S. Naval Air Station, Dutch
Harbor, Alaska.

No witnesses not otherwise connected with the investigation were present.

The recorder was called as a witness by the recorder and was duly sworn.

Examined by the board:

1. Q. State your name, rank, and present station.

A. Jay S. Anderson, Lieutenant Commander, U. S. Navy, recorder of this board.

2. Q. Are you the legal custodian of the original navigation chart used by
the S-27 at the time of grounding? If so, produce it.

A. I am. Here it is.

The chart was submitted to the defendant and to the board and by the recorder
offered in evidence for the purpose of entering into the record, appended
hereto marked "Exhibit 1." There being no objection, it was so received.

3. Q. Are you the legal custodian of the rough log book of the S-27?

A. I am. Here it is.

The log was submitted to the defendant and to the board and by the recorder
offered in evidence only for the purpose of reading into the record such extracts therefrom as show the location and movements of the S-27 from 17 June
1942 to 19 June 1942 and the officers serving on board during that period.
There being no objection, it was so received.

4. Q. Refer to that log and read such portions thereof as pertain to the
facts for which it has been offered in evidence.

The witness read from the said log pertinent extracts, copy appended marked
"Exhibit 2".

5. Q. Are you the legal custodian of the night order book?

A. I am. Here it is.

The night order book was submitted to the defendant and to the board and by
the recorder offered in evidence. There being no objection it was so received, copy appended marked "Exhibit 3".

None of the parties to the investigation desired further to examine this
witness.

The witness resumed his seat as recorder.

A witness called by the recorder entered, was duly sworn, and informed of the
subject matter of the investigation.

Examined by the board:

1. Q. State your name, rank, and present station.

A. Richard Philip Nicholson, Lieutenant, U. S. Navy, attached to and serving
on board the U.S.S. S-28. -3-

2. Q. Have you worked up the reckoning of the S-27 from the data obtained from her navigation officer to enable the board to fix the true position of the ship at the time of her taking aground?

A. I have, within the limitations available.

3. Q. What are these limitations?

A. The limitations in establishing the true position of the S-27 are as follows: it was found that for the period immediately prior to the grounding, two possible and probable tracks could have been traversed. Within my powers of decision it has been impossible to definitely state which tract was traversed.

4. Q. Is this included in your report?

A. It is.

5. Q. Have you the navigational plot and work in writing?

A. I have.

6. Q. Produce it.

A. Here it is, sir.

The navigational plot and report were submitted to the defendant and to the board and by the recorder offered in evidence. There being no objection, they were so received, copies appended marked "Exhibit 4" and "Exhibit 5", respectively.

7. Q. Was the position of the ship accurately ascertained at the last opportunity?

A. I can't answer that directly. The last terrestial fix obtained is equally applicable to either of the two tracks previously mentioned. The terrestial fix on either track cuts in within reasonable limits of accuracy.

The court examined the work and requested further details from the witness, who then being duly warned, withdrew.

At 12:00 noon the board recessed until 2:00 p.m., at which time it reconvened.

Present: All the members, the reporter, the defendant and his counsel.

No witnesses not otherwise connected with the investigation were present.

A witness called by the ~~recorder~~ board entered and was warned that his previous oath was still binding.

Examined by the ~~recorder~~ board:

1. Q. State your name, rank, and present station.

A. Frank McElhany Smith, Lieutenant, U. S. Navy, navigator of the U.S.S. S-27.

2. Q. Will you please state to the board everything within your knowledge relating to the matter under investigation?

-4-

A. Beginning with the afternoon we had come around the island, we were taking cuts from noon on, on a basis of going around the island and had been getting

pretty good cuts, although there was difficulty at times in identification.
The visibility was changing, sometimes we could not see the entire island,
sometimes I could see peaks in the distance. We rounded the island, I had
picked up the -- the right tangent was clear at all times. As we cut around
on the south side there was a doubt as to the left tangent until on the
second observation, I think, I picked up another left tangent, far left tangent, coming out. I had plotted bearings in two places on the chart and compared them with visibility of the distances at which I thought they were, and
settled on the tangent in the point that I was cutting on. From then on, the
cuts were consistent and good. The last cut that I got was about 1735, I
think. After that I didn't get any more. When we surfaced there was nothing
in sight that I could get a cut on. I took a look around and I had asked the
Quartermaster and the O.O.D. to let me know if at any time they saw anything
I could cut on. During the evening I went ahead and turned in for a while.
I had gotten up about 2330, I think, to decode a message. I was in the process of decoding this when I heard the ship start bumping. I started for the
bridge. I was going into the control room, I think, and I ran into the chief
of the watch at the door going to the captain's stateroom. I went on to the
bridge and went up on the bridge. The captain was right by me. He had come
out of the stateroom just after I had gone by the door. I think I asked the
officer of the deck, "What's the trouble?" He said, "We have hit rocks or
something". The captain took the deck at that time. I remember the engines
-- the motors, rather, were backing. After we stopped from the initial back
emergency I looked around. The rocks on the starboard side were two groups.
I don't know whether I saw both those groups at that time or only the one.
They were right by the bridge. From then on we backed and twisted at various
combinations. The starboard screw was reported out of order at -- sometime
after we had started our maneuvering. As we backed down, the stern would back
into a reef and ride up a little bit, and then shear to starboard. It was
light enough, I think, at this time, that we could see another set of rocks
that were just off the starboard quarter and on several occasions the stern
got close or practically against these rocks and we kicked ahead. We couldn't
do any good with this maneuvering so we stopped for a while and took a lead
all around the ship -- soundings. They were all very shallow except dead
ahead there was one spot, at twenty or thirty feet, but there was apparently
another reef beyond. I was on the bridge all the time except for a few in-
spections below decks. The stern was pounding on the rocks. The bilge
plating in the motor room was buckled in. You could notice it coming in when
you were in the motor room when she pounded. After this had been noticed and
I thought the limit had been reached on the motor room, we secured this,
closed the door and put a pressure on it. During this time the makeup of
radio messages was going on. I don't remember the process. Lieutenant Butler
was encoding them. Not long after the -- or after the first few maneuvers,
Lieutenant Butler had started gathering confidential material together to
destroy. Along about four o'clock we decided to send somebody ashore. We got
the boat up and sent one officer and one of the men ashore in a boat. From
then on, the pounding seemed to get worse and worse. The swells would lift
the ship up considerably and she would strike on the starboard side and pound
again to port plenty fast. There was no period of a long roll between pounding. The seas were breaking over the boat pretty heavy and kept increasing
during the morning. During the morning we sent off the rest of the men and
each boat took in some provisions, clothing, and miscellaneous gear, and confidential papers to be burned. The last few trips were pretty rough. Waves
were breaking all the way across the boat and would fill it up on the starboard
side before you could get it away from the ship. In the afternoon, after the
next to the last boat had left, the captain and I coded one or two messages to
send. I remember the last one, I think the radio man was having considerable
trouble with the transmitter on the last one. By that time on deck, why the
waves were breaking across the bow. The last boat, the radio man and myself
were in, alongside the conning tower, and the captain hauled it forward to
the torpedo room right by the bow to get in the boat so we could leave the
ship clear of rocks. At the time there was very little freeboard at the bow.
She was down at the bow -- there was just six to twelve inches of freeboard
with the stern up considerably. From there we went on shore and established
a camp on the beach in a cove.   - 5 -

3. Q. How was the last fix obtained and at what time?

A. It was a right tangent of Amchitka and a left tangent and tangent in between -- it's mostly a left tangent. At that time I could almost see down the left side of it.

4. Q. I show you this chart. Do you recognize it?

A. I do.

5. Q. What is this chart?

A. It is a chart including Amchitka Island which I used in navigating at the time of the grounding.

6. Q. Is this the largest scale chart available of the area?

A. Yes, it is the best chart available.

7. Q. Is this the chart furnished by the Navy Department for navigating in this area?

A. It is.

8. Q. What is the description of this chart?

A. It is a preliminary chart to the Alaskan Aleutian Islands, Rat Island, Kiska Island, to Semisopochnoi Island, from U. S. survey in 1935. It is a confidential chart, number 5640, serial number 469, issued to the Commanding Officer, U.S.S. S-27, dated 11 May 1938.

9. Q. Is it corrected up to date?

A. It is corrected up to date.

10. Q. What is the last notice to mariners entered?

A. The last confidential notice to mariners entered was number three, 1938.

11. Q. Is that the last one that has been issued?

A. To the best of my knowledge, it is.

12. Q. At what time on June 18 did you make your landfall?

A. On June 18 it was around five o'clock in the morning.

13. Q. You may refresh your memory by any of these records here if you wish.

A. We sighted the island at 0504 and were able to get a cut until 0556.

14. Q. What zone times are these?

A. These are all plus twelve.

15. Q. You got your fix at--?

A. 0556.

16. Q. Were you able to obtain a fix all during the day?

A. Some time on we had a fix, usually every half hour. The last -- there were one or two times we did not get one. - 6 -

17. Q. What was the last fix you obtained prior to the grounding?

A. The last fix was at 1735 June 18.

18. Q. The last fix was obtained at 1735, is that correct?

A. Yes.

19. Q. Why were you unable to get a fix after that time?

A. We were unable to see any land, apparently due to a fog bank close to the land.

20. Q. Then after 1735 you were not able to see land?

A. No, sir.

21. Q. What set and drift of current did you note between 0556 and 1735 in the evening?

A. During the morning we had maneuvered and had not picked up any definite set. When we started around the end of the island there was considerable set in a southeasterly direction. As we turned westward after passing the end of the island the set -- I was getting fairly long bearings. When I got in closer I noticed a decidedly northwesterly set. After about two or three cuts it increased and we decided to turn south and speed up considerably to get back down. We turned up here (indicating on the chart). These three cuts were pretty good set and the next cut showed a decided set of increased intensity. The cuts at 1635 and 1703 showed an apparently northerly or northwesterly set increasing as we would come along. We turned south about that time or shortly after.

22. Q. What description of the currents of this area is contained in the Coast Pilot for the area?

A. There is no information on the currents other than breakers have been reported about eight miles south and east of East Cape, and the Coast Pilot, in a general statement of the Aleutian Islands, says that in addition to the lack of surveys, navigation in this region is made difficult by the prevailing thick weather and further by the lack of knowledge of the currents which obtain considerable velocity at times, and that all passages in the Aleutian Islands have strong currents. On account of the scarcity of reliable observations, definite current predictions cannot be made. The effect of the tidal currents has often been felt offshore at a considerable distance from the passes, resulting in unexpected sets, and a vessel is in more danger there from the currents than from any other except the lack of surveys. Those statements were from the U. S. Coast Pilot, Alaska, part two, fourth edition, of 1938.

23. Q. What were your course and speeds after the time of the last fix?

A. After the last fix at 1735 we continued on 240 true at two and one-half knots until 1736. At 1736 we changed course to 270 degrees true and speed of four knots. At 1759 we changed to 180 degrees true, speed of six knots. At 1806 we changed to 240 at six knots. At 1820 we changed course to 270 true. At 1915 we changed course to 210 true. At 1920 we surfaced. At 1925 we went ahead two thirds on both engines, eight knots. At 1929 we changed course to 315 degrees true. At 2005 we stopped. At 0027 on the nineteenth we went ahead two thirds on starboard engine on course 305 at six knots. This was the course and speed up until the time that land was sighted close aboard and the O.O.D. was coming left to 225 and backing shortly after sighting land.

-7-

24. Q. Did you make an eight o'clock position report?

A. We had worked it out on a chart.

25. Q. How did you determine the fix?

A. It was by D.R. run up from the 1735 fix.

26. Q. Did you apply any current between the 1735 fix and the 2000 position?

A. The D.R. plotted on the chart was without current. I had applied current to see about where I could possibly be if set or current were affecting me.

27. Q. You told me how long you stopped. It was about four hours, wasn't it?

A. We stopped from 2005 to 0027.

28. Q. What allowance did you make for drift during the time you stopped?

A. I had run back about as I remember it was one knot. I had just taken a circle on the chart to see roughly where I might be. I had not plotted a position on the chart using a set.

29. Q. Did you take any soundings at any time?

A. No soundings were taken.

30. Q. What sort of apparatus had you aboard for taking soundings?

A. We had hand lead for soundings only. There was no fathometer aboard.

31. Q. And no sounding machine?

A. There were no facilities for taking soundings in this water. During the afternoon all the set that I had experienced had been north or northwesterly and I would consider it as tending to put my actual position more toward where we wanted to be.

32. Q. What was the bearing and distance of your D.R. position at the time of grounding from the spot where you actually grounded?

A. The position of grounding as determined by reconnaissance was eight point seven miles bearing zero eight four and one-half from my D.R.

33. Q. What was your set and drift?

A. The drift was one point two knots. The set was zero eight four and one-half.

34. Q. How does this compare with the previously experienced currents?

A. The drift was approximately the same as I expected. The set was about 150 degrees difference.

35. Q. You expected about that amount of current but you expected it in the other direction?

A. Yes, sir. However, I had taken into account that if there were a set to the east we were far enough around Makarius Point to take care of it.

36. Q. Did you notice any tide rips such as are seen in Akutan or Unimak Pass as you rounded East Cape?   - 5 -

A. At one time when we were still on a southeasterly course the helmsman remarked on the fact that she seemed to be carrying more rudder than usual. I was considering that we had considerable southeast current and attributed it to this.

37. Q. Was the sea choppy from tide rips or smooth?

A. The sea was notparticularly choppy but heavy swells.

38. Q. In other words, you noticed current not from the state of the sea but from the way the ship was handling?

A. From the ship and the fixes.

39. Q. Did you at any time consider the courses as set to be dangerous? Was there ever any doubt in your mind as to the safety of the course as steered?

A. No immediate danger. When we were getting a northwesterly set south of East Cape, we considered that this course, had it been continued any length of time, would --

40. Q. What do you mean, this course?

A. A northwesterly course. We considered that a northwesterly course might have carried us closer to the island than we desired to be. Therefore we changed south.

41. Q. How long did you continue south?

A. We were on a course of south or southwest for a total of about forty-five minutes.

42. Q. Were there any available radio direction finder shore stations?

A. There were none.

43. Q. Does the ship have a radio direction finder?

A. The ship does not have a radio direction finder.

44. Q. Do you have any sound equipment that would enable you to determine the ship's position?

A. We have a Q.C. sound equipment. It was being used at the time of the grounding, according to our prescribed policy on patrol.

45. Q. What is that policy?

A. The J.K. side of the equipment was being used for listening. The policy was to listen only and use the J.K. This part of the equipment cannot be used for echo ranging. When standing a listening watch it is used because of its greater sensitivity.

46. Q. Did you have equipment that would have allowed you to have received an echo range from shoals?

A. It might. We have equipment which we can echo range upon shoals.

47. Q. Why was this not being used?

A. When on patrol we should not use echo ranging equipment because of disclosing our position.

48. Q. Do you have orders to this effect?

-9-

A. No definite orders never to use it that I know of.

49. Q. When, before the grounding, were you last able to make a celestial observation?

A. I had made no celestial observations for several days prior because of availability of land fixes and lack of celestial objects and low visibility.

50. Q. What was the state of the tide at the time of grounding?

A. I do not know. There is no tide data available for this vicinity.

51. Q. Did you make any tidal observations after the ship grounded? Did you notice what the rise and fall was?

A. We noticed that high tide appeared to be roughly around midnight and low tide around noon. The rise and fall appeared to be about two feet.

52. Q. Do you keep a book in which you record all of your observations and computations for the purpose of navigating the ship?

A. I keep a book for bearings and a work book for celestial observations.

53. Q. Can you produce them?

A. I can produce the bearing book but the work book was not salvaged.

54. Q. What compasses did you carry?

A. We had a gyro and a magnetic.

55. Q. When was the error of the gyro last observed?

A. The error of the gyro was zero. The gyro had been overhauled at the Bremerton Navy Yard on 26 May 1942.

56. Q. What means do you have for observing compass error?

A. By bearings.

57. Q. Can you take an azimuth of the sun, for instance?

A. By an azimuth of a celestial body.

58. Q. When was the last observation made?

A. By bearings the morning of the eighteenth.

59. Q. Describe what you mean by determining the error by bearings.

A. If three identified objects are cut, the error is considered zero.

60. Q. When was the last sun azimuth taken?

A. It was several days prior to the grounding. Records showing these observations were not salvaged and no opportunity for an azimuth occurred between our run from Adak to Amchitka. We did not have a corrected table of deviation.

61. Q. Have you a magnetic compass?

A. Our magnetic compass was entirely unreliable. I had no deviation tables.

62. Q. Had you ever attempted to compensate your magnetic compass?

A. I had.

- 10 -

63. Q. Do you have a comparison compass check book?

A. We keep a compass check book.

64. Q. Can you produce it?

A. It was not salvaged from the boat after grounding.

65. Q. Why do you consider the magnetic compass to be unreliable?

A. All attempts to compensate this compass since the ship was wiped had failed.

66. Q. What was the draft of the ship fore and aft?

A. Prior to grounding the draft forward was about seventeen feet six inches and draft aft was about twenty-one feet six inches. These drafts are approximate.

67. Q. How were they taken? How do you know what your draft is after you have been at sea so long?

A. The boat was in diving trim, but number three main ballast tank was full of fuel, thereby causing her to be much heavier aft when on the surface.

68. Q. Why did you say that the compass was no good after the ship had been wiped?

A. There was a strong magnetic south pole in the periscope shears. We found no compensation which we could use that would bring the compass back to normal. At the time of the grounding I had a magnet in front of the compass which caused it to be approximately correct but not consistent.

69. Q. Did you have available the Pilot Chart for the Pacific for June, 1942?

A. We did not have one available, sir.

70. Q. Had you made an effort to obtain one before departing on the cruise?

A. They usually arrive in the mail -- to the best of my knowledge they were not out when we left on the cruise.

71. Q. What is the general set and drift of the Kamchatka branch of the Japan stream in this vicinity?

A. In this vicinity it is east northeast about one-half knot.

72. Q. Did you take cognizance of this current in your calculations?

A. I considered that we were more under local tidal influences and did not.

73. Q. Using the tide tables for 1942, will you tell the board the time of high and low tide at the nearest reference to your point of grounding for this date?

A. The tide at Kiska Harbor would have been high at 1937 on the eighteenth of June, zone twelve time. The next low tide would be at 1224 on the nineteenth.

74. Q. Please tell the board how bearings are taken when a submarine is submerged.

A. The periscope is trained on the object and when on, a mark is taken. The gyro heading is read by the helmsman on this mark and is applied to the periscope bearing, which is relative.   -//-

75. Q. How long have you been the navigating officer?

A. I have been the navigator on the S-27 for about six months. This is my only navigation experience.

76. Q. Had you noticed any erratic performances of the gyro previous to the groundings?

A. None since leaving Seattle on this cruise.

77. Q. In taking your bearings on the southern part of Amchitka Island, how clearly defined were the tangents which you used?

A. The tangent was recognizable within a degree but the lower part was well below the horizon.

78. Q. There were no better navigational aids to use?

A. There were no better navigational aids available.

The board then at 4:40 p.m. adjourned until 9:00 a.m. tomorrow.

-12-

SECOND DAY

U. S. Naval Air Station,
Dutch Harbor, Alaska.
Thursday, July 2, 1942.

The board met at 9:00 a.m.

Present: Commander Charles C. Phleger, U. S. Navy, member;
Lieutenant Commander Thomas C. Thomas, U. S. Navy, member; and
Lieutenant Commander Jay S. Anderson, U. S. Navy, member, and
acting as recorder;
Anthony C. Tarr, Civil Service CAF-6, reporter;
Lieutenant Commander Herbert L. Jukes, U. S. Navy, defendant,
and his counsel.

The record of proceedings of the first day of the investigation was read and
approved.

The board was cleared. The board was opened. No witnesses not otherwise connected with the investigation were present.

At this stage of the proceedings it appeared to the board that Lieutenant
Frank McElhany Smith, U. S. Navy, was a defendant. He was accordingly called
before the board and advised to that effect, and of the declarations that
seemed to implicate him. He examined the convening order, stated that he did
not object to any member of the board, and was informed of his rights. He
introduced Lieutenant Commander J. D. Crowley, U. S. Navy, as his counsel.

The witness decided to continue his testimony at his own request, and was informed that his previous oath was still binding, and that his examination
would be governed by the same rules as govern the examination of an accused
who takes the stand at his own request in a trial by court martial.

Examined by Lieutenant Commander Jukes, defendant:

79. Q. What duties did you perform in addition to those of navigator?

A. Besides navigator, I was first lieutenant, gunnery officer, torpedo officer,
aid to the executive officer, and stood watches as watch officer.

80. Q. In what status was the S-27 when you received orders to leave your
mainland base?

A. We were in an overhaul status at San Diego.

81. Q. How long after receipt of these orders did you depart from your mainland base?

A. We received orders on the eighteenth of May and departed on the twentieth
of May.

82. Q. Did these orders indicate your destination?

A. Only as the northern portion of the Pacific.

83. Q. What opportunity did you have for detailed navigational preparations
for this cruise?

A. Very little. I was mainly concerned with getting the ship back to a sea-
going condition from the overhaul status and obtaining necessary supplies.
We had all torpedoes in the shop under overhaul when the orders were received
and a great portion of the machinery of the boat was broken down for overhaul.

-13-

84. Q. Did these requirements of getting the boat operative require all your time before departure from San Diego?

A. Practically all my time was necessary for these items.

85. Q. Is the effect on the magnetic compass of wiping a constant one or a variable one?

A. It is a variable effect due to change of latitude and to the tendency of the magnetic condition of the ship to return to its normal condition over a period of time after wiping.

86. Q. You stated in the direct examination that you did not have deviation tables for the magnetic compass. Will you please elaborate on that statement?

A. I had no deviation tables for the compass in its present condition. I had deviation tables for the compass prior to the wiping of the ship. These tables were on board and were checked frequently but were plainly in error.

87. Q. Shortly after the vessel was wiped, did you swing for compensation or residuals?

A. We did.

88. Q. Please state the result of that effort at compensation?

A. On the first effort the compass would maintain only one heading even for any amount of compensation available. On the second effort larger and more magnets were available but failed to provide satisfactory compensation.

89. Q. What magnetic course did the compass indicate on first compensation?

A. About three four zero degrees on all true headings.

90. Q. Did the second compensation or the second effort at compensation show any great improvement?

A. It showed very little improvement.

91. Q. Did you consult any navigators of other vessels or any other competent persons as to the possible corrections or corrective measures for this condition?

A. I consulted the navigator and the captain of the S-28 and my own captain. The S-28 was having similar difficulty in compensation. No method had been found by which proper compensation could be effected.

92. Q. Was this situation recognized in the submarine force of the Pacific fleet and by the bureau?

A. It was. There were various letters from forces afloat and from bureaus stating that compensation would probably be difficult as there had been no precedent. They requested that anyone finding a method of compensation describe this method to the bureau.

93. Q. What were the limits of your assigned patrol area?

A. The area to which we were proceeding was between bearing zero nine zero and one two zero true from North Head, Kiska Harbor.

94. Q. When was this area assigned to you?

A. It was assigned at the time we left patrol off Adak. I do not know the date.

- 14-

95. Q. Did you have any opportunity to inquire into local knowledge of piloting in the waters of that area?

A. I did not.

96. Q. Your only sources of information were those in publications on board?

A. They were.

97. Q. How far off the south coast of Amchitka Island was the southern limit of your area?

A. It was about three to four miles.

98. Q. During what part of the day were you running submerged on the day prior to the grounding?

A. We dove at 0207, surfaced about 1920.

99. Q. What consideration dictated this submerged running?

A. We considered ourselves in an area very likely to be patrolled by enemy air or surface forces, therefore adhered to an established policy of diving before daylight and surfacing about dark.

100. Q. Does equal opportunity exist when submerged and when on the surface for making celestial observations?

A. It does not. There is no opportunity submerged for making celestial observations.

101. Q. Does equal opportunity exist for making terrestial observations?

A. Not equal opportunity. Observations by periscope are limited by the time available, by ease of taking, and by limits of visibility.

102. Q. Can you leave your periscope exposed continually in an area of this kind?

A. You can not.

103. Q. How frequently were observations made on the day preceding the grounding?

A. About every twenty to thirty minutes.

104. Q. What other observations other than navigational were required on each periscope exposure?

A. The primary purpose of the exposure was search for enemy forces. This was done as soon after exposure as possible. Navigational data was obtained upon exposure as long as it did not hinder the search problem. If any unidentified ship or plane was sighted, procedure for approach was necessarily paramount to navigation.

105. Q. What forces had control of the air and surface to the best of your knowledge at that time in that vicinity?

A. We considered it likely that there were more enemy forces present than friendly.

-16-

106. Q. Your last terrestial fix was obtained at 1735 on June 18. Were frequent periscope exposures continued after this time?

A. Yes.

107. Q. Was anything sighted on any periscope exposure after this time?

A. Nothing was sighted after seventeen thirty-five.

108. Q. Why was the island not visible?

A. There appeared to be a haze or fog bank between us and the island.

109. Q. Did you consider that your track along the southern side of Amchitka Island was dictated solely by navigational considerations or primarily by military requirements?

A. The track was necessary from a military standpoint. We had discussed the fact that we would not be in this vicinity except for the military necessity.

110. Q. Then your entire estimate of the navigational situation was colored by the known military requirements?

A. It was.

111. Q. You stated in direct examination that no azimuth was obtained for several days prior to grounding. Did any opportunity exist for taking an azimuth during this time?

A. To the best of my knowledge, there was no opportunity.

112. Q. Was that because of submerged running or that no objects were visible?

A. There were no objects visible for a proper azimuth.

Examined by the board:

113. Q. To your knowledge is it the doctrine of submarines when patrolling on the surface in the vicinity of land to patrol as near as possible to shore to avoid Radar detection?

A. It has been the policy of our boat to stay about five miles from land at night or any other time that we might be charging.

114. Q. I show you these air photographs. Do you recognize them?

A. I do.

115. Q. What are they?

A. They are pictures of the S-27 after grounding.

The photographs were submitted to the defendants and to the board and by the recorder offered in evidence and placed in the record, appended marked "Exhibit 6".

116. Q. What is your opinion concerning the possibility of salvaging this ship?

A. It could conceivably be done over a long period of time with considerable equipment and no hinderance from enemy operations.

− 16 −   None of the parties to the investigation desired further to examine this witness.

The board informed the witness that he was privileged to make any further statement covering anything relating to the subject matter of the inquiry which he thought should be a matter of record in connection therewith, which had not been fully brought out by the previous questioning.

The witness stated that he had nothing further to say.

The witness was duly warned and resumed his seat as defendant.

At 11:15 a.m., the board recessed until 1:00 p.m., at which time it reconvened.

Present: All the members, the recorder, the parties to the investigation and their counsel.

No witnesses not otherwise connected with the investigation were present.

Lieutenant Smith, defendant, with the permission of the board, introduced Lieutenant Commander J. E. Stevens, U. S. Navy, as his counsel, vice Lieutenant Commander Crowley, who continued to act as counsel for Lieutenant Commander Jukes.

A witness called by the recorder entered, was informed of the subject matter of the investigation, and warned that his previous oath was still binding.

Examined by the board:

1. Q. State your name, rank, and present station.

A. T. E. Krueger, Boatswain, U. S. Navy, U.S.S. S-27.

2. Q. Were you the officer of the deck at the time of the grounding of the S-27?

A. Yes, sir.

3. Q. Will you please state to the board everything within your knowledge that bears on the grounding of the boat from the time that you came on watch until after the grounding of the boat?

A. I relieved Ensign Young on the deck at about midnight that night. Visibility was fairly low, about half a mile or so, I would say. I had read the captain's night order book in which he left orders that when they had finished charging the batteries we were to go ahead at two thirds speed about six knots on the one engine and continue the charge on the other engine and set course three zero five, keeping a special lookout for land, and if I suspected any land in the vicinity to change course to two two five. About twenty five minutes after twelve the watch below reported they had finished charging on both engines and I went ahead two thirds speed on the starboard engine on course three zero five. About five or ten minutes after that, they requested permission to start charging air with the starboard air compressor, which I granted. At the time that we went ahead at two thirds speed and came to three zero five, the fact was reported to the commanding officer. At about 0045 I and the quartermaster on watch both sighted a darker looking cloud about a point off the starboard bow which I took to be land. At this time I ordered the helmsman, who was below, to change course to two two five and also to report to the captain that I believed I had sighted land and that I was coming to two two five with full left rudder. As I straightened up from passing the word down the hatch, I noticed breakers just ahead of the bow and I immediately rang up back engines on both motors. A few seconds after that we hit, and about the same time the captain came on the bridge and took charge. After that we continued backing on the motors until we found we

-17-

couldn't clear. We also went ahead on the motors to clear the stern and somewhere along in there the starboard screw was disabled and we only had the port screw left to maneuver with. Evidently we hit on the rocks astern. When we found that the ship couldn't be pulled clear of the rocks or couldn't maneuver it clear of the rocks, the captain sent a message reporting his position and predicament, and about five o'clock we sent the rubber life boat ashore with two men. Just after we struck and the captain came on the bridge, we started blowing the tanks dry and lightening the ship as best we could. From five o'clock on until around about eleven o'clock we continued transferring men and provisions to the beach with the rubber life boat. I think I left the ship some time around eight thirty or nine o'clock. I guess that is about all as far as the grounding is concerned.

4. Q. Would you tell the board what information you received from your relief -- from the officer of the deck that you relieved, relative to the dangers of navigating?

A. He passed on the word that if we sighted any ship or planes to dive immediately and he also had told me to keep a lookout for land. Of course I had read all that in the captain's night order book.

5. Q. Is it possible or practicable to have an anchor ready to let go on a submarine?

A. Well, yes, sir, it is possible.

6. Q. Is there an anchor ready for letting go?

A. Well, a submerged anchor could have been let go within a minute and a half or two minutes, I would say.

7. Q. In your opinion, would it have been possible -- from the time of sighting land -- to let the anchor go?

A. No, sir.

8. Q. Were lookouts posted?

A. Yes, sir, we had two lookouts, one on port side and one on starboard, and the quartermaster on the bridge was also acting as a lookout.

9. Q. How far from the land were you when you first saw it?

A. I would say about a quarter of a mile, sir, probably not that far.

10. Q. That wasn't the land you struck, was it?

A. No, sir, that was steep bluffs in back of it.

11. Q. We have here some small photographs. Do you recognize them? If so, tell the board.

A. Yes, sir, these are all pictures of the boat where she is now lying.

12. Q. What boat?

A. The S-27, sir.

13. Q. In a grounded position?

A. In a grounded position, yes, sir.

-18-   The photographs were submitted to the board and to the defendants and by the recorder offered in evidence. There being no objection, these photographs were so received and appended marked "Exhibit 7".

14. Q. Tell the board in as much detail as possible the material condition of the boat after grounding or when last boarded.

A. Well, the only thing I have to go on there is, about two days before the last boarding, I think it was, I went aboard and the torpedo room was completely flooded. Before we had left the ship, the ballast tanks had ruptured.

15. Q. We have in mind the possibility of salvaging the boat. Will you tell us what material condition she is in from what you have observed?

A. I do not believe it is salvageable, myself.

16. Q. I would like you to elaborate on that.

A. I noticed air bubbles leaking out of the ballast tanks and I also know that the torpedo room was flooded because I looked through the eye port from the forward battery compartment. From the pounding that we took on the motor room before we kicked ahead and cleared the rocks, I would say that the structure of the stern of the boat would be materially weakened. Right after I was up in the torpedo room the captain came aboard and he found chlorine gas in the forward battery, which would indicate that the forward battery well was punctured. The day after that we sent a man over with a boat and while he was there the gases from the forward battery lifted the auxiliary induction intake valve from its seat, which indicates an internal pressure.

17. Q. Tell us something about the rocks around the ship. How badly is she on?

A. There is a submerged rock on the port beam. I do not know how large it is but it must be fairly good size because we couldn't get over it and then astern there is another rock that was submerged and that's the one that we must have gone in over that we couldn't get back over again. Then on the starboard side there are two large reefs both about fifteen or twenty feet long. Then ahead you have got the main shore line of the island. There are large rocks dead ahead of the ship that are separated from the shore. There is a little water ahead of it before it gets to the main part of the island.

18. Q. What kind of bottom is there in that area?

A. Right where the ship is, it is rock, sir. They are rather worn from the sea. From the way we slid up and off of them all the time, I would say they are rounded. The surface of them is pretty jagged, that's the parts that are above the water.

19. Q. Has the heading of the ship changed since she went on?

A. Not very much, sir.

20. Q. Is the ship in the same position in these photos taken June 29 as she was when she went aground on the nineteenth? In other words, has she been moved by the sea?

A. I would say she is about in the same position she was when I last saw her except she may be a little farther down by the bow.

21. Q. What was the course of the ship when she struck?

A. I don't exactly know because we were changing course at the time, but I think it was about two eight zero. The reason I don't know what the ship's head was is because the bridge was darkened and there was no light in the compass.

—19—

22. Q. Did you inform yourself of the position of the ship before going on watch?

A. Yes, sir.

23. Q. Where did you believe the ship to be when you went on watch?

A. About five or six miles west of Saint Makarius Point.

24. Q. Did you have a leadsman in the chains?

A. No, sir, it is impractical to have a leadsman in the chains on a submarine because of the low freeboard. He is liable to get washed overboard.

25. Q. Did you sound a collision signal?

A. I didn't personally but the watch below did.

26. Q. Was this signal sounded before the ship struck?

A. I would say it was sounded about the same time.

27. Q. How much experience have you had as an officer of the deck on a submarine?

A. Well, I didn't start standing deck watches until we left Seattle, but I had stood instruction watches with Mr. Smith all the way from San Diego up to Seattle, and on top of that all my time in the Navy, practically, has been on the bridge as quartermaster.

28. Q. You have received your warrant recently?

A. Yes, sir, I got it the day before we left San Diego.

29. Q. What do you estimate the speed of the vessel through the water just before you ordered emergency astern?

A. About six knots, sir.

30. Q. Did you consider this a safe speed as regards to the visibility then existing?

A. Yes, sir.

31. Q. Are you acquainted with the type of damage done to the propeller? Was the engine itself destroyed?

A. I believe the starboard shaft leading to the propeller was bend out of shape so it would not turn any more.

32. Q. Is it customary to steer in the control room at night time at sea?

A. Well, it has been since we went to war, sir.

33. Q. In your opinion, can the torpedoes be taken off?

A. I don't think so, sir, due to the torpedo room being flooded and the vessel being down by the bow.

-20-

34. Q. In your opinion, can the boat be salvaged?

A. Well, it could be, I suppose, if you had pontoons and a couple of tugs up there and didn't have any outside interference from the enemy. However, I don't believe the ship would float if the pontoons were not fastened on to it before it was pulled off the reef.

Examined by Lieutenant Commander Jukes, defendant:

35. Q. Was the vessel rigged for diving when you came on watch?

A. Yes, sir, it was rigged for diving and I had inspected it before I came on watch.

36. Q. Did you run rigged for diving at all times when at sea in war time?

A. Yes, sir.

37. Q. What is the average diving time for the K-27?

A. I would say about a minute, sir.

38. Q. Would it have been possible to have a leadsman on deck without necessarily slowing down your diving time?

A. No, sir.

39. Q. Would it have been safe under the conditions of the sea existing to have a leadsman on deck?

A. No, sir. Well, inasmuch as I thought we were six miles away from Saint Makarius Point, I would not have put a leadsman in the chains.

40. Q. Did you have any apprehension of being dangerously close to land before having sighted it?

A. No, sir, I didn't. There is something else -- making six knots on the surface that way, even if you had a leadsman in the chains, he would not be able to get a sounding that would be of any value. He isn't far enough above the water to get a good swing on the lead for one thing, and the result is that the lead would only go a short distance ahead and by the time it got abeam of him it would still be down only about twenty or thirty feet.

Examined by Lieutenant Smith, defendant:

41. Q. Do you know why you were making six knots?

A. Yes, sir. I know that we wanted to reach our patrol area at Kiska Island as soon as practicable and we could make better time on the surface than we could submerged. That is, any sustained speed, and six knots is about the best we can do on one engine.

Examined by Lieutenant Commander Jukes, defendant:

42. Q. What is the minimum speed you could make on one engine?

A. About five knots, one third speed.

43. Q. You stated that the air compressor was on the starboard shaft. What is the most efficient engine speed for operating that compressor?

A. It is about two thirds speed on one engine, or six knots.

44. Q. Then the military requirements of making best speed to patrol area and recharging the air banks for the next day's diving dictated a speed of six knots?

-21-

A. That is correct, sir.

A. Well, it could be, I suppose, if you had pontoons and a couple of tugs up there and didn't have any outside interference from the enemy. However, I don't believe the ship would float if the pontoons were not fastened on to it before it was pulled off the reef.

Examined by Lieutenant Commander Jukes, defendant:

35. Q. Was the vessel rigged for diving when you came on watch?

A. Yes, sir, it was rigged for diving and I had inspected it before I came on watch.

36. Q. Did you run rigged for diving at all times when at sea in war time?

A. Yes, sir.

37. Q. What is the average diving time for the S-27?

A. I would say about a minute, sir.

38. Q. Would it have been possible to have a leadsman on deck without necessarily slowing down your diving time?

A. No, sir.

39. Q. Would it have been safe under the conditions of the sea existing to have a leadsman on deck?

A. No, sir. Well, inasmuch as I thought we were six miles away from Saint Makarius Point, I would not have put a leadsman in the chains.

40. Q. Did you have any apprehension of being dangerously close to land before having sighted it?

A. No, sir, I didn't. There is something else -- making six knots on the surface that way, even if you had a leadsman in the chains, he would not be able to get a sounding that would be of any value. He isn't far enough above the water to get a good swing on the lead for one thing, and the result is that the lead would only go a short distance ahead and by the time it got abeam of him it would still be down only about twenty or thirty feet.

Examined by Lieutenant Smith, defendant:

41. Q. Do you know why you were making six knots?

A. Yes, sir. I know that we wanted to reach our patrol area at Fisks Island as soon as practicable and we could make better time on the surface than we could submerged. That is, any sustained speed, and six knots is about the best we can do on one engine.

Examined by Lieutenant Commander Jukes, defendant:

42. Q. What is the minimum speed you could make on one engine?

A. About five knots, one third speed.

43. Q. You stated that the air compressor was on the starboard shaft. What is the most efficient engine speed for operating that compressor?

A. It is about two thirds speed on one engine, or six knots.

44. Q. Then the military requirements of making best speed to patrol area and recharging the air banks for the next day's diving dictated a speed of six knots?

-21-

A. That is correct, sir.

Examined by the board:

45. Q. Did you verify the data in your log for this particular watch?

A. Yes, sir, as a matter of fact I wrote it in.

46. Q. Did the visibility differ materially between 0000 and 0100 that night?

A. It did not until just before we ran aground there, and I think that was probably fog off the land. However, things were happening fast there.

47. Q. You have entered in the log for 1:00 a.m. that the visibility was point three, which is objects not visible at three hundred yards, is that correct?

A. Yes, sir, I entered it that way.

48. Q. Do you know at the speed you were making at the time just before the accident, how far your ship could go before it could be stopped at emergency back?

A. At emergency back I think it would stop within two hundred yards.

49. Q. On one or two engines?

A. That is backing on both, sir.

None of the parties to the investigation desired further to examine this witness.

The board informed the witness that he was privileged to make any further statement covering anything relating to the subject matter of the investigation which he thought should be a matter of record in connection therewith, which had not been fully brought out by the previous questioning.

The witness made the following statement:

In regards to the condition of the boat -- of course, this does not have any value as far as salvaging it is concerned -- that is, your starboard stern plane is missing. That was after the grounding.

The witness was duly warned and withdrew.

A witness called by the recorder entered, was informed of the subject matter of the investigation, and was warned that his previous oath was still binding.

Examined by the ~~recorder~~ board:

1. Q. State your name, rate, and present station.

A. Dick Demont Lister, signalman first class, attached to U.S.S. S-27.

2. Q. Were you the quartermaster on watch on the bridge at the time of the grounding of the S-27?

A. Yes, sir, I was.

3. Q. Tell the board everything within your knowledge just prior to the grounding of the S-27 while you were on watch.

-22-

A. I came on watch at midnight and relieved the watch. It was pretty dark and foggy. There was two charging batteries on both engines. About twenty-five minutes after I came on watch the charge on the starboard engine was secured and we went ahead two thirds on course three zero five true. Suddenly the lookout and myself and the officer of the deck all sighted land at the same time on the starboard bow and the officer of the deck sent word to the captain and gave the order for the wheel to come left to two two five. Just about that time we hit the rocks. The captain came to the bridge and took charge.

4. Q. Can you give any more details?

A. No, sir, that's all up to the time we struck. The officer of the deck -- as soon as we felt the bump, we rang up emergency astern on all engines and the alarm was sounded. The O.O.D. had already given the order to come left to two two five true.

5. Q. Were there any other men or officers on watch in addition to the officer of the deck and the lookout and yourself?

A. There was myself and the officer of the deck and two lookouts.

6. Q. What is your estimate of the distance away that land was sighted ahead?

A. The land sighted was just a dark shape. I would say about three hundred and fifty to four hundred yards, in my estimation.

7. Q. What was the state of the sea?

A. The sea was very calm and it was very foggy.

Examined by Lieutenant Smith, defendant:

8. Q. Were the lookouts equipped with binoculars?

A. Yes, sir, at all times the lookouts and the quartermaster and the O.O.D. all had binoculars.

9. Q. Would you tell us why you steered below decks instead of on the bridge?

A. I think the main reason was because there was so many men to get down the hatch. If there was a surprise we would have to clear the bridge as rapidly as possible. It would eliminate one man getting down the hatch.

None of the parties to the investigation desired further to examine this witness.

The board informed the witness that he was privileged to make any further statement covering anything relating to the subject matter of the investigation which he thought should be a matter of record in connection therewith, which had not been fully brought out by the previous questioning.

The witness stated that he had nothing further to say.

The witness was duly warned and withdrew.

A witness called by the recorder entered, was informed of the subject matter of the investigation, and was warned that his previous oath was still binding.

Examined by the board:

1. Q. State your name, rate, and present station.

-23-

A. Arthur Dallas Kenner, chief electrician's mate, U.S.S. S-27.

2. Q. Were you the control man on watch at the time of the grounding of the
S-27?

A. Yes, I was, sir.

3. Q. Tell the board everything within your knowledge at your station, the
orders you received and the performance of the machinery, any abnormal thing
that you observed.

A. I took the watch at midnight and we were charging batteries on both
engines. At twenty-five minutes after twelve we secured the charge on the
starboard engine and went immediately on the screw and were charging air on
the same screw and charging batteries on the port engine. At 0043 by the
control room clock there was a loud bumping that sounded like we raised up
over something. Of course I could not see anything and emergency astern was
rang at the same time and I answered the bell in a few seconds. The collision alarm was also sounded. For an indefinite period we were backing emergency and had the different bells. We backed emergency to start with and
the bells were changing from then on.

4. Q. What was the condition of the control room the last time that you saw
it? What date was that?

A. It was on the nineteenth, sir. In the afternoon of the nineteenth and it
was quite a mess, sir.

5. Q. What do you mean by a mess?

A. The J.K. and the Q.C. had all been torn apart and everything was distrib-
uted through the control room. Some clothing and provisions were laying
around in the control room that we couldn't get off. We didn't run our starboard motors. Of course, the port motor was ready at all times and I stayed
on the station.

6. Q. When you got the first backing bell, which engines did you back?

A. I backed on the port motor first, sir, and it wasn't but a few seconds
that we had both motors going back on emergency.

7. Q. As you recall, what was the relation in time between striking the reef
and the backing of the two engines?

A. It was a matter of seconds, sir.

8. Q. Do you mean you struck first?

A. By the time they got the clutch all lined up it was only a matter of a
few seconds.

9. Q. Did you strike the reef before you backed?

A. That's kind of hard to say, sir.

Examined by Lieutenant Commander Jukes, defendant:

10. Q. How long do you estimate the first emergency backing bell to have
been?

-24- A. A period of three or four or five minutes. But we were backing on different bells for a period of two and a half hours, I would say.

Examined by the board:

11. Q. You mean --

A. After we struck we continued backing and going ahead and trying to get off the rocks for a period of two and a half hours.

Examined by Lieutenant Commander Jukes, defendant:

12. Q. How much gravity did you have?

A. We had about eleven fifty-five gravity, sir.

13. Q. What is bottom gravity?

A. About ten eighty is bottom gravity for power.

14. Q. What is bottom gravity for power of the order required to give you emergency astern?

A. For emergency astern you should have almost full gravity, sir.

15. Q. Can you estimate gravity for me there?

A. I would say eleven fifty gravity there for emergency astern and stay with it for any length of time.

16. Q. Were there indications toward the end of your backing that the screws were then coming out of the water?

A. Yes, sir, they were. My ammeters would go from fifteen hundred to three thousand a side and tried to hold it to three thousand as long as we were backing emergency.

17. Q. Then with one screw disabled and the other one kicking out of water, there was not much further that could be done with the screws toward getting the vessel off?

A. That's right, sir.

None of the parties to the investigation desired further to examine this witness.

The board informed the witness that he was privileged to make any further statement covering anything relating to the subject matter of the investigation which he thought should be a matter of record in connection therewith, which had not been fully brought out by the previous questioning.

The witness stated that he had nothing further to say.

The witness was duly warned and withdrew.

A witness called by the recorder entered, was informed of the subject matter of the investigation, and was duly sworn as an expert witness.

Examined by the board:

1. Q. State your name, rank, and present station.

-25-

A. Carl E. Anderson, Lieutenant Commander, D-V(S), U. S. Naval Reserve, and I am now ordered for duty at the Naval Air Station, Dutch Harbor. I am also

Commander of the Aleutian Patrol.

2. Q. Would you give us a brief of your sailing experience in the Aleutian Islands?

A. I have navigated the Aleutian Islands since 1913. As master, as navigator in naval vessels in 1918, 1919, and 1920. As master of my own vessels and other vessels in 1921, 1922, 1923, 1924, and 1925. Also master of vessels trading out there in 1932, 1933, 1934, and 1935. For the Navy again in 1940, 1941, and 1942.

3. Q. Are you familiar with the waters around the island of Amchitka?

A. I am.

4. Q. What current would you expect to encounter around the island of Amchitka about the eighteenth of June?

A. I will expect to encounter a current from the southeast to the northwest or from the northwest to the southeast.

5. Q. Can you tell us a little more about the currents that you might expect in that region? What is the effect of tidal currents?

A. The tidal currents there in a flood tide will set you north and west on the flood tide. They will set you south and east on an ebb tide, but it is not necessary that those things will happen. I have been out in those Aleutian Islands where I have had the current both in the flood tide and ebb tide setting in the same direction for as much as twenty-one days.

6. Q. How do you account for that?

A. Wll, in the spring of the year the ice comes out of the Arctic and it forces the whole body of water down towards the Pacific. Then later on when the ice melts, that body of water goes back into the Bering Sea. That's the only way I can figure it, because when you have the ice coming out in the spring it happens in the latter part of May and the first part of June. You have always a southerly current from the Bering Sea into the Pacific. Then later on when this has disappeared and the Bering Sea is clear of ice, it seems that the water feeds back again into the Bering Sea, but more so if you have a flood tide you will have an easterly or a westerly and a northerly set and on the ebb tide you will have a southerly and an easterly set.

7. Q. By a flood tide you mean flooding into the Bering?

A. By flood tide I mean the tide is rising. For instance, you have a flood tide off on the north side of Unimak Island or Unalaska Island here. Now you will have from here, say, from between Cape Cheerful and Cape Korinska, you will have an easterly set on your ebb. From Cape Korinska on to Unimak Pass you will have a westerly set on your ebb tide. On the flood you will have the same thing and they will meet on the outside of Ronky Point there.

8. Q. The movement of the flood water is from the Pacific into the Bering?

A. Yes, sir.

9. Q. Are you familiar with the tide tables?

A. Yes.

-26-

10. Q. Do ~~you think you could compute~~ *you believe you could compute* the time of high tide at Amchitka from reference to the tide tables?

A. No, I was never able to.

11. Q. What differences have you noted?

A. Well, I have seen the tide -- out there, you know, sometimes you will have two high tides and two low tides in twenty-four hours and other times you will have only one in twenty-four hours -- one high and one low water in twenty-four hours. I don't think there are any regulations as far as tides out there. You take False Pass, for instance. The same thing any place where you have the heavy currents you have in these passes. I don't think you can figure the tides out. When I go out there I generally check up the tide for instance at Kiska, and make a note in my log book to that effect and I figure six and a half hours. If I have a high tide at noon I will have a low tide at six thirty in the evening. I have found that around new moon and full moon you will have two tides and around in the middle, like in the first quarter and the third quarter, when the current is not so strong, they will run longer. In other words, on these -- around, say, for instance, on the first quarter or last quarter they probably will run twelve hours one way and twelve hours the other way. On the new and full moon they will run six hours or something like that. It takes from high water to high water thirteen hours and from low water to low water thirteen hours, during the new and full moon. At new and full moon it is pretty nearly impossible for anybody to figure the currents out there. After you have been out and noticed them for some time you can keep a little track of the tides in the Aleutians in the first and last quarters.

12. Q. From your experience, has the tide data proven to be true?

A. From my experience nothing that I have tried to figure out in the Aleutians has ever been true. I don't believe that the tide data for Dutch Harbor is correct.

13. Q. What current would you expect to encounter during a flood tide on the southeast coast of Amchitka Island? It is flooding and you are down around Saint Makarius Point.

A. I would expect a northwesterly current.

14. Q. Up the island?

A. Yes, sir, very much so.

15. Q. How much, in general terms?

A. In general terms on ordinary tides, one and a quarter to one and a half knots northwest set.

16. Q. What would you expect on the northeast side of the island?

A. On the northeast side on a flood tide I would expect the tide to set me through the northwest along the island and if I am at Saint Kamaga Point I would be set into the island and up. If I am on this side down in here (southeast side) I would expect to be set to the eastward and away from the island on an ebb tide. If I am over here some place on an ebb tide I would be set away from the island and over this way. On a flood tide I would be set up this way and in towards the island. That's what I would expect.

17. Q. I show you these pictures. Do you believe that the submarine whose pictures you see there could be salvaged?

- 27-

A. No, sir, I don't believe it could be salvaged. That is a major job and it is very seldom that you have enough weather there that you could -- that submarine will break up. One good southeasterly gale and she will break up.

18. Q. I show you a chart (appended marked "Exhibit 1"). What is your opinion as to the accuracy of this chart?

A. It is good.

19. Q. Is there a larger scale chart available of Amchitka Island?

A. No, sir, this is the largest scale chart available for the rest of Amchitka, except for a larger scale chart of Constantine Harbor.

Examined by Lieutenant Commander Jukes, defendant:

20. Q. Would you expect a navigator who is on his first trip to the Aleutians and had only the publications available, to make any correct estimate of the currents to be encountered in the Amchitka area?

A. No, sir.

21. Q. You have described the currents that might generally be encountered, but would you expect these conditions to hold on any given day?

A. No. They are likely to vary at any time. I don't think any man living knows the currents out there. During these foggy periods it would be impossible for anyone to keep a correct plotting of his position except that he dropped his anchor and laid there, and at that you might drag.

22. Q. Then you would consider it dangerous from a navigational standpoint for a vessel to operate within the confines of this area for a long period of time?

A. Yes, sir, very dangerous.

None of the parties to the investigation desired further to examine this witness.

The board informed the witness that he was privileged to make any further statement covering anything relating to the subject matter of the investigation which he thought should be a matter of record in connection therewith, which had not been fully brought out by the previous questioning.

The witness stated that he had nothing further to say.

The witness was duly warned and withdrew.

At 4:45 p.m. the board adjourned until 9:00 a.m. tomorrow.

—28—

THIRD DAY

U. S. Naval Air Station,
Dutch Harbor, Alaska.
Friday, July 3, 1942.

The board met at 9:00 a.m.

Present: Commander Charles C. Phleger, U. S. Navy, member;
Lieutenant Commander Thomas C. Thomas, U. S. Navy, member; and
Lieutenant Commander Jay S. Anderson, U. S. Navy, member, and
acting as recorder;
Anthony C. Tarr, Civil Service CAF-6, reporter;
Lieutenant Commander Herbert L. Jukes, U. S. Navy, defendant,
and his counsel;
Lieutenant Frank McElhany Smith, U. S. Navy, defendant,
and his counsel.

The record of proceedings of the second day of the investigation was read
and approved.

No witnesses not otherwise connected with the investigation were present.

A witness called by the recorder entered, was informed of the subject matter
of the investigation, and warned that his previous oath was still binding.

Examined by the board:

1. Q. State your name, rate, and present station.

A. S. I. Jorgesen, seaman first class, U.S.S. S-27.

2. Q. Were you the starboard lookout on or about the time of the grounding
of the S-27?

A. Yes, sir.

3. Q. State to the board everything within your knowledge, what you saw, and
anything that might be of help in this investigation.

A. Well, sir, I was starboard lookout and went on watch at twelve o'clock
and it was foggy when I went up there -- misty -- and visibility was poor at
the time, fairly good other times -- sometimes one thousand yards or a
little less. Then it became practically zero at other times. It seemed
like the fog was in patches but it was mostly foggy all the time. When we
ran into one of these heavy patches, we saw a large black piece of -- it was
sort of like a big dark cloud was ahead of us, and at that time I saw
breakers and reported to the officer of the deck that I saw the breakers and
shortly after or right after that we started hitting on the rocks. Then we
went on them. That's all.

4. Q. Were you using binoculars?

A. No, sir, we couldn't use them because the mist had fogged them up so much
we couldn't see through them.

5. Q. Did you say that you were in a dense fog patch at the time you saw the
land?

A. Yes, sir, I would say there was one or two hundred yards visibility,
probably.   -29-

5. Q. How soon after you sighted land did the ship turn away from its course?

A. We were swinging away from the course when I sighted land. I believe we were making a turn when we sighted.

None of the parties to the investigation desired further to examine this witness.

The board informed the witness that he was privileged to make any further statement covering anything relating to the subject matter of the investigation which he thought should be a matter of record in connection therewith, which had not been fully brought out by the previous questioning.

The witness stated that he had nothing further to say.

The witness was duly warned and withdrew.

A witness called by the recorder entered, was informed of the subject matter of the investigation, and warned that his previous oath was still binding.

Examined by the board:

1. Q. State your name, rate, and present station.

A. Robert Ashley Shirah, seaman first class, from the S-27.

2. Q. Were you the port lookout on or about the nineteenth of June at the time of the grounding of the S-27?

A. Yes, sir.

3. Q. Tell the board everything within your knowledge, what you saw, and anything else that might be of interest to the board.

A. Well, when I came on lookout at eleven o'clock that night, we were running into fog banks. It wasn't a steady fog, sometimes we could see farther than other times, and at that particular moment we were involved in one of those fog banks. Visibility was very low. It had been reported to the officer of the deck that visibility was down. Nothing was in sight. I was to the seaward. There was no land. I wasn't given any notice to look out for land on the seaward side in particular.

4. Q. Have you anything further that you remember?

A. No, sir, there is nothing else of importance, sir, that I remember. It was just a natural watch.

5. Q. Didn't you see the land before the ship struck?

A. No, sir, there was such a terrible fog bank, all I was noticing was on the port lookout side and I hardly ever noticed the starboard lookout side.

6. Q. Did you have binoculars?

A. Yes, sir.

7. Q. Could you use them?

A. No, sir, the mist would make it impossible to use binoculars.

8. Q. What were the lighting conditions just before the ship struck? That is to say the natural lighting outside -- was it light or dark?

- 30 -

A. It was very dark, sir.

None of the parties to the investigation desired further to examine this witness.

The board informed the witness that he was privileged to make any further statement covering anything relating to the subject matter of the investigation which he thought should be a matter of record in connection therewith, which had not been fully brought out by the previous questioning.

The witness stated that he had nothing further to say.

The witness was duly warned and withdrew.

The court navigator, Lieutenant Richard Philip Nicholson, was recalled by the recorder, informed his previous oath was still binding, and his work was re-examined by the board.

Examined by Lieutenant Commander Jukes, defendant:

1. Q. You show two possible tracks after the 1230 fix. These are based on a purely academic plot of recorded bearings of tangents, and not analyzed in the light of practical factors such as estimated distance off shore, conture of shore line, and interpretation of various visible but unidentified high points?

A. Yes.

2. Q. At the time that you had progressed in your analysis to the 1735 fix, what was the trend of currents established?

A. The trend of currents established were as follows: considering the inside tangent, point six five knots toward one four six degrees true; considering the outside tangent, point nine four knots toward one seven eight degrees true.

3. Q. That is for the entire period 1230 to 1735, is it not?

A. That is for the entire period 1113 to 1735. 1113 is the origination of the analysis.

4. Q. You have also analyzed currents between each of the various fixes obtained in this period?

A. Yes.

5. Q. Were they constant?

A. No.

6. Q. What was their general trend?

A. In breaking down the analysis of currents between successive fixes, considerable variation both in direction and amount was found. No continuity either in acceleration or deceleration of strength or changes of directions of currents was established.

7. Q. At the time of the 1735 fix were you prepared to forecast currents that might be expected in the next six or eight hours?

A. No.

Examined by Lieutenant Smith, defendant:

- 31 -

8. Q. Did the ship's position relative to Amchitka Island appear to have any effect on the currents found?

A. Yes. In considering the two possible tracks as shown on the chart, the inside track for a period of analysis of two hours and forty minutes, between 1455 and 1735, showed a general trend set to the northeastward. The outside track for the same period showed a general set to the northwestward.

Examined by the board:

9. Q. What has been your navigation experience in the Western Aleutians?

A. For a period of approximately fourteen days while on war patrol in the vicinity of Kiska Island on the U.S.S. S-28.

10. Q. What is your opinion of the problem facing a submarine navigator in these waters?

A. The problem facing a submarine navigator in my opinion is most difficult.

11. Q. What is your opinion of the accuracy of cross bearings taken by a submerged submarine on tangents on an unfamiliar coast and plotted on a chart of the scale of the chart you are using?

A. In my opinion the accuracy and identification of such points is always dubious.

12. Q. Do you think that is why you found such variation in so-called currents? In other words, isn't it probable that the reason you could find no constant trend in currents between fixes is because the fixes themselves are not true fixes?

A. That is possible but in my opinion the relationship of the East Cape of Amchitka Island to Amchitka Pass could be very apt to cause uncertain eddies and currents in the general vicinity of that position. In analyzing the currents as derived from the tracks of the S-27, it was my opinion that the variations in currents derived could have and probably did exist.

13. Q. Then you believe it is more probable that there were irregular currents than that the fixes themselves are inaccurate?

A. As shown in previous testimony, the fixes could have been based upon either of two sets of origins. Not having been with the S-27 at the time, it is impossible for me to give an opinion as to the accuracy of the identification of these points. In regard to the currents, it is my opinion that the variations shown could have been actually existent. I can make no relative comparison between accuracy of fixes or accuracy of currents.

14. Q. In putting your two tracks on this chart you spoke of some of the bearings not fitting the tracks. Which of the two tracks had the greater number of fixes which fitted?

A. Both tracks were equally accurate in this respect. As the bearing book shows, numerous bearings were occasionally taken, identification of which has been impossible. It was found that the two tracks could be fitted in, in all respects equal as to number of bearings tracing the track of the vessel along that track.

None of the parties to the investigation desired further to examine this witness.

The board informed the witness that he was privileged to make any further statement covering anything relating to the subject matter of the investigation which he thought should be a matter of record in connection therewith, which had not been fully brought out by the previous questioning.

-32-

The witness stated that he had nothing further to say.

The witness was duly warned and withdrew.

A witness called by the recorder entered, was informed of the subject matter of the investigation, and was duly sworn.

Examined by the board:

1. Q. State your name, rank, and present station.

A. Burton G. Lake, Commander, U. S. Navy, commanding Submarine Division 41.

2. Q. What duty was being performed by the S-27 on the cruise in question?

A. The S-27 had entered Dutch Harbor on the twelfth of June for fuel and provisions. She departed in the early morning of the thirteenth with orders to proceed to her patrol station in the vicinity of Kiska Island. After the departure from Dutch Harbor, the patrol station was changed so that the S-27 patrolled for about two days north of Adak Island, then proceeded to a sector, the limits of which were bearings zero nine zero to one two zero from North Head, Kiska Harbor. There were no outer limits to this patrol area but the orders were to take maximum offensive action against the enemy known to be at Kiska and to patrol as close to the region as practicable. During the time that the S-27 was in Dutch Harbor for fuel, I told the commanding officer that I would like to have him make a reconnaissance of Constantine Harbor, Amchitka Island, on the way to his station and also, if practicable, the eastern end of Amchitka Island, to determine if there were any enemy activities in that vicinity.

3. Q. What are the existing orders or the policy on such a patrol governing the use of sound gear?

A. The S-27 is one of the vessels in the division which has keel mounted sound equipment. This equipment is used at all times submerged and should be used at all times on the surface at night or in extremely low visibility. This is echo ranging equipment and normally the echo ranging feature would not be used if there was any possibility of its giving away the submarine's location to the enemy, but only the listening feature would be used to detect the approach of vessels at night or in low visibility. No positive orders have been issued as to how this equipment is to be used, but I believe that is the general policy throughout the submarine -- in all submarines. It is left to the discretion of the commanding officer as to how he will use his equipment in any particular circumstances.

4. Q. Would you consider the echo ranging feature available for navigation under the circumstances that existed on June 18?

A. I think it would depend entirely on what the commanding officer had previously observed in that area and whether or not there was any doubt in his mind as to navigational problems and the urgency of the circumstances which might require the use of the equipment for echo ranging. There shouldn't have been any hesitancy in using the equipment for navigational purposes. The range of this equipment for navigational purposes is usually rather limited.

5. Q. I show you this chart on which certain cross bearings taken on tangents have been plotted by a submerged submarine. In your opinion would it be possible for the submarine to accurately fix its position in this manner on an unfamiliar coast at a distance of about five miles from the beach where no known navigational marks exist, and considering the small scale and lack of detail on the chart?

-33-

A. If the bearings were taken accurately, I think it would probably fix the position of the ship within a mile or a mile and a half. It would depend entirely on the number of tangents available to take bearings on.

6. Q. As division commander, have you investigated the material condition of the S-27 since grounding?

A. Yes, as far as possible.

7. Q. Do you believe that she can be salvaged under the present circumstances?

A. Under the present circumstances I do not believe that the S-27 can be salvaged. I think it would require the best possible salvage equipment and uninterrupted work over a considerable period under good weather conditions to salvage the S-27.

8. Q. Do you consider it a safe policy to stop for a period of four or more hours for charging batteries as close as five miles from land in this particular area under conditions of poor visibility?

A. I don't think it is safe to stop in a position five miles from land for five hours and then assume at the end of the five hours that the movement of the ship could be continued without taking very careful consideration as to the currents. I don't think the fact of stopping that close to land is in itself dangerous but upon getting under way due consideration should be given to the currents which may have carried the ship out of position during the time she was stopped.

9. Q. I show you a plot made by the court navigator. He has been unable to determine from plotting cross bearings which of two tracks the ship might have been on. Do you believe that there could be any doubt existing in the ship itself as to which of the two tracks they were on? In other words, he doesn't know which tangents they used. He gets good cuts on both tracks. Could you tell in a submerged submarine whether you were ten miles or five miles from the beach by observation of the shore line?

A. I don't think you could tell off Amchitka Island because there aren't any landmarks there to judge distance by.

10. Q. Are you familiar with this coast of Amchitka?

A. Yes.

11. Q. What is the nature of the land there?

A. A high, rocky beach and the land itself is almost entirely flat. I don't believe there are any landmarks there that could be used other than tangents. In judging distance from land through the periscope I think it might be difficult off this island to tell how far you were from land.

12. Q. The previous testimony has stated that the torpedo room of the S-27 is flooded. Do you believe it would be possible, under the circumstances that exist, to remove the torpedoes from the S-27?

A. I do not believe the torpedoes can be removed for the same reason that I do not believe the ship can be salvaged, namely because it would require a considerable period of uninterrupted work with adequate salvage equipment.

13. Q. I show you some photographs of the S-27 as she was on June 29. Do you believe that a vessel in such position, considering your knowledge of weather in this locality, would remain in good condition very long?

- 34 -

A. I think that the ship will probably break up in the next severe storm in that area if the wind is from the south, and probably the damage due to pounding is becoming progressively worse even in moderate weather. My reason for saying that the torpedoes cannot be salvaged is because I don't believe the enemy would give you the opportunity to do it, not because I don't think it could be done with adequate equipment and good local weather.

14. Q. I show you the S-27 navigator's 2000 position on June 18. Is that position within the assigned sector for this vessel?

A. That is not in the sector to which he was assigned. However, he was authorized to disregard sector limits in proceeding to attack the enemy and he was also directed to make a reconnaissance of the east end of Amchitka Island if practicable.

15. Q. Then the decision of the S-27 to proceed to its patrol area via the west coast of Amchitka Island was a proper decision as far as you were concerned?

A. I don't know why the commanding officer decided to proceed via the west coast of Amchitka. Personally, I would have proceeded via the northeast coast. From my knowledge of the currents through the passes between Rat Island and Amchitka Island, I should prefer to go in the deep water northeast of Amchitka Island. But I see no objection to the S-27 proceeding along the southwest coast if he preferred to go that way.

Examined by Lieutenant Commander Jukes:

16. Q. Would you consider that the commanding officer of the S-27 was carrying out his mission if he did not accept the lack of aids to navigation and manifest dangers of navigating so close to land in areas of uncertain current in order to accomplish the reconnaissance and attempt to get to his patrol station as quickly as possible, assuming, of course, that every precaution consistent with proceeding as quickly as possible was exercised?

A. In order to carry out his mission it was necessary for him to approach close enough to see if there were any ships in Constantine Harbor or any signs of extensive enemy activity on the island itself. I consider five miles as a reasonable distance under good visibility conditions for such a reconnaissance.

17. Q. Do you consider that completely recharging the batteries every night is a military necessity?

A. Yes.

18. Q. Even though it is necessary to lie to, to complete the charge?

A. Yes.

19. Q. After seventeen and one quarter hours of submerged running and with about six hours of darkness available for charging, is it necessary to lie to with this type of submarine in order to complete the charge before daylight?

A. Yes. But it is not necessary to lie to during the entire charging period.

None of the parties to the investigation desired further to examine this witness.

The board informed the witness that he was privileged to make any further statement covering anything relating to the subject matter of the investigation which he thought should be a matter of record in connection therewith.

-35-

64

which had not been fully brought out by the previous questioning.

The witness stated that he had nothing further to say.

The witness was duly warned and withdrew.

At 12:05 p.m. the board recessed until 1:30 p.m., at which time it reconvened.

Present: All members of the board, the recorder, the defendants and their counsel.

No witnesses not otherwise connected with the investigation were present.

A witness called by the recorder entered, was informed of the subject matter of the investigation, and warned that his previous oath was still binding.

Examined by the board:

1. Q. State your name, rate, and present station.

A. Charles Orville Wolber, gunner's mate first class, U.S.S. S-27.

2. Q. Were you the chief of the watch at the time of the grounding of the S-27?

A. Yes, sir.

3. Q. Tell the board everything within your knowledge with relation to the subject in question, which is the grounding of the S-27.

A. I took the watch over at twelve o'clock and we were laying to charging batteries. We secured the starboard engine at about twenty-five minutes after twelve and went ahead on course three zero five, I believe. In just a few minutes -- I would say two or three minutes before they hit -- they sent down word to change course to the left at full left rudder and come to two two five and report to the captain that he thought he had sighted breakers on the starboard bow, which I did, and the captain got up and went to the bridge right away. We hit about the same time along there, is about all that happened. The rest of the time I took orders from the bridge and carried them out.

4. Q. Did you get orders from the bridge to sound collision quarters?

A. I don't remember. It was sounded down below. The chief electrician's mate sounded that. I closed the main and auxiliary induction in the meantime. I believe word came down, yes, sir.

5. Q. What are the duties of the chief of the watch?

A. He dives the boat on orders, closes the inductions, opens the Kingstons, operates the trim individual and trim pump, pumps the water in the variable tanks.

Examined by Lieutenant Commander Jukes, defendant:

6. Q. You mentioned in your testimony that you called the captain. Is that part of your duties as chief of the watch?

A. Yes, sir.

7. Q. Does making that call remove you from the control room, which is your principal station?   - 36 -

A. No, sir, your ward room is right there. You can holler right into the staterooms.

None of the parties to the investigation desired further to examine this witness.

The board informed the witness that he was privileged to make any further statement covering anything relating to the subject matter of the investigation which he thought should be a matter of record in connection therewith, which had not been fully brought out by the previous questioning.

The witness stated that he had nothing further to say.

The witness was duly warned and withdrew.

A witness called by the recorder entered, was informed of the subject matter of the investigation, and warned that his previous oath was still binding.

Examined by the board:

1. Q. State your name, rate, and present station.

A. Scott Eddy Horton, seaman first class, present station submarine base, Dutch Harbor.

2. Q. Were you on watch as steersman of the S-27 at the time of the grounding?

A. Yes, sir, I was.

3. Q. Tell the board everything within your knowledge about what you remember about the grounding.

A. Well, a few minutes before the grounding I was steering course three zero five. Word came to the bridge left full rudder, course two two five. That was approximately two minutes before the crash. I was coming left to two two five when the crash occurred. After the crash occurred I don't know exactly what course the boat stopped on but it never reached my course to come left at two two five.

4. Q. What heading did she stop on?

A. At approximately two eight five.

5. Q. Approximately two eight five?

A. Yes, sir.

6. Q. What compass were you steering by?

A. The gyro repeater, sir.

7. Q. Were you applying any correction to your gyro heading on three zero five?

A. No, sir. It was true.

8. Q. How long after you got the order to come left at full rudder did you turn the steering control?

A. Just immediately, as soon as word came from the bridge, sir.

9. Q. When you are running on one engine like that, does the ship turn readily or not?

A. Yes, sir, it did on this occasion.

-37-

Examined by Lieutenant Commander Jukes, defendant;

10. Q. What is the normal procedure for checking the compass against the gyro on the S-27?

A. The electrician has charge of checking the compass and he gives the order to stand by for compass check and someone checks through the gyro and I check the gyro repeater at the word "mark". This is marked on the ship's head and is entered in the electrician's log. The course and the error both, the gyro and the gyro repeater.

11. Q. How frequently is this done?

A. Every thirty minutes.

12. Q. Are the results reported to the bridge?

A. No, sir, they are not.

13. Q. If there is any discrepancy, are the results reported to the bridge?

A. Yes, sir.

Examined by the board;

14. Q. What time did you come on watch?

A. At twelve o'clock, sir.

None of the parties to the investigation desired further to examine this witness.

The board informed the witness that he was privileged to make any further statement covering anything relating to the subject matter of the investigation which he thought should be a matter of record in connection therewith, which had not been fully brought out by the previous questioning.

The witness stated that he had nothing further to say.

The witness was duly warned and withdrew.

Lieutenant Commander Herbert L. Jukes, defendant, requested to be sworn as a witness and was warned that his previous oath was still binding and was informed by the board that his examination would be governed by the same rules that govern a defendant called at his own request in a trial by court martial.

Examined by Lieutenant Commander Jukes, defendant;

1. Q. What information of enemy forces in the area east of Kiska Island did you have on the eighteenth of June?

A. During our passage from Adak to Amchitka we had broken down several messages concerning task force eight and the information therein indicated that the enemy forces, that is seaplanes, other planes, and surface vessels, were present in there in the vicinity of Kiska Harbor. Also the information gained from the messages led me to believe that there might be enemy forces at Semisopochnoi Island.

2. Q. You were proceeding to the eastern end of Amchitka Island to reconnoiter this area for possible enemy installations. Did this make you feel that there were possible enemy forces in that area?   —38—

A. Yes. I did not believe that I would have been ordered to reconnoiter in that area unless there had been indications of enemy activity.

3. Q. Did you make any contacts during the day of June 18?

A. During the forenoon and while reconnoitering Constantine Harbor, a plane was sighted bearing north, distance about eight to ten miles and about fifteen degrees of elevation. We immediately went to deep depth and remained there for about a half hour.

4. Q. Please tell the board now you felt you must operate your ship and make your periscope observations under these circumstances.

A. Under these circumstances and with the clear water found in this area, I felt that periscope exposures should be made every twenty or thirty minutes with the minimum of time for exposure consistent with a good look, and then remain at seventy or eighty feet until time for another exposure.

5. Q. How long had you been running on offshore submerged patrol during the period immediately preceding June 18?

A. With the exception of two days, I had been running an offshore patrol for a period of sixteen days. These sixteen days had been spent in submerged patrol at entrances to Cold Bay and entrances to Kuluk Bay.

6. Q. Do you feel that during this period you acquired a good perspective for estimating and evaluating the distances of land objects with a periscope?

A. With an average of eighteen hours a day of submerged operations with periscope exposures at least every thirty minutes, and being at all times during this period able to see landmarks, I feel that I can safely say that I had become sufficiently used to the periscope and observing landmarks to have been able to judge my distance within reasonable limits. Most of these exposures were made both in low power, which gives a magnification of only one point five, and in high power, which gives a magnification of six.

7. Q. Based upon your estimated distance off the southeast corner of Amchitka Island on the afternoon of June 18, coupled with your evaluation of the visible contour of the shore line, which of the two probable tracks described by the court navigator do you feel that you were on?

A. I feel certain that I was on the outside track, that is, at least four to five miles from the shore. From observations in the morning when I had deliberately closed Constantine Harbor, to within two miles, and the observations in the afternoon using the same periscope magnification, there was a very appreciable difference in the nearness of the beach. In fact in the afternoon with the periscope in low power, the beach at times was hardly discernable.

8. Q. Without any knowledge whatsoever of the height of the shore line, your ability to discern detail such as vegetation, et cetera, on the shore, affords a good estimate of distance, does it not?

A. When within one to two miles of the shore, vegetation and so forth are quite readily seen. I have never been able to discern any growth on an island at a greater distance.

9. Q. Were any of the above described details visible on Amchitka Island during the afternoon of June 18?

-39- A. There were not. The only visible thing was the contour of the bluff at each tangent and possibly the higher points in the background.

10. Q. Did you recognize the possibility at the time of there having been two possible positions, and take this possibility into consideration?

A. Yes. At about two o'clock when the cut was plotted in the two positions, this possibility was discussed with the navigator and we both used the periscope in order to help us make our decision as to which was the correct track.

11. Q. Then the possibility of two positions as obtained from cross bearings of tangents was recognized and you decided that you were at the outer of the two positions after considering the features we have just discussed?

A. That is correct.

12. Q. Your last fix was obtained at 1735 on June 18. Did you make frequent periscope exposures subsequent to that time?

A. Periscope exposures were continued at intervals varying from twenty to thirty minutes after the last fix was obtained, until the moment of surfacing.

13. Q. Did you personally conduct some of these exposures?

A. I personally conducted the great majority of the exposures.

14. Q. Did you at any time see land subsequent to 1735?

A. Subsequent to 1735, no land was visible. Just before 1735 I noticed and remarked upon the fact that our afternoon haze was closing out our beach.

15. Q. Were you on the bridge immediately after the vessel was surfaced?

A. Within thirty seconds after the surfacing. I was the second man on the bridge. The first man on the bridge was the quartermaster, whose duties were to open the hatch, immediately climb to the highest point and take a quick look in all directions. I followed him within a space of five seconds after the hatch was opened.

16. Q. What were the light and visibility conditions at this time?

A. As stated in my narrative, the visibility was from two to three miles. The sky was completely overcast, but it was not dark.

17. Q. If stars would have been available that night, you were in a position to have gotten them?

A. Yes.

18. Q. Had you noticed the currents that had affected your vessel during the afternoon?

A. Yes. Immediately after each tangential fix the navigator and I would try to determine in which direction we might be getting set. That is why the decision was made to turn south and southwest and increase speed.

19. Q. Were you able to find any consistent indications upon which you could forecast currents to be expected during the night?

A. No.

Examined by Lieutenant Smith, defendant:

20. Q. Was there any land in sight when you surfaced?　　　　－40－

A. There was no land in sight when we surfaced.

Examined by the board:

21. Q. What was the draft before grounding?

A. The approximate draft before grounding was seventeen feet six inches forward and twenty-one feet six inches aft.

22. Q. What was the draft after grounding?

A. The approximate draft after grounding was seventeen feet three inches forward and seventeen feet aft. The draft after grounding was not well determined due to blowing of tanks.

23. Q. What was the list?

A. Even keel before and after grounding.

24. Q. Give a general distribution and amounts of variable weights before grounding.

A.
Forward trim tank	9,000 pounds.
Auxiliary tank	32,000 pounds.
Regulator tank	Dry
After trim tank	Full of fresh water, 11,800 pounds.
Number three main ballast	5,000 gallons diesel, 4,000 gallons salt water.
Battery water tank	530 gallons.
Fresh water tank	1,000 gallons.
Forward fuel group	4,264 gallons.
After fuel group	5,313 gallons.
Number nine fuel oil tank	6,171 gallons.
Main lub oil tank	780 gallons.
Reserve lub oil tank	1,300 gallons.
Main drain	Flooded.

Provisions in normal stowage.
Four torpedoes in tubes - not flooded.
Eight torpedoes in racks.

25. Q. Give a statement of compartments flooded and rapidity of flooding.

A. No compartments flooded immediately after grounding. Three hours, estimated, after grounding, auxiliary tank began slow leakage. Eight hours, estimated, after grounding, number one and number two main ballast tanks began slow leakage. Sixteen hours, estimated, after grounding, torpedo room began flooding slowly. Completely filled sometime during next twenty-four hours. Seventy-two hours, estimated, after grounding, forward battery flooding slowly. The cause of all flooding was considered due to damage to structure (seam leakage) resulting from heavy pounding.

26. Q. What was the material condition of readiness in effect at time of grounding?

A. The ship was rigged for diving with the following exceptions: Conning tower hatch open; main induction open; auxiliary induction open. All watertight compartments doors were open but were closed immediately after grounding.

27. Q. Give a summary of steps taken to control damage and to correct list or trim.

A. Ship was rigged for collision. All watertight doors were closed. Number three main ballast tank was blown dry. Forward and after trim tanks were .

-41-

blown dry. Forward and after fuel groups were blown dry. Number nine fuel tank was pumped to five thousand gallons. High pressure pump was started on motor and engine room bilges. Motor room was abandoned and pressure put in compartment due to buckling of bilge plating.

28. Q. State any failure or especially effective performance of material installations.

A. All material installations performed in a satisfactory manner. Structural damage occurred only after prolonged extremely heavy pounding.

29. Q. How long have you been commanding officer of the S-27?

A. I had been in command of the U.S.S. S-27 for a period of six weeks.

30. Q. Was this your first submarine command?

A. This was my first submarine command.

31. Q. Was the officer of the deck at the time of grounding qualified to have the deck?

A. Yes.

32. Q. During the night of June 18-19, were the required reports made to you by the officer of the deck?

A. Yes. To the best of my knowledge.

33. Q. Were you informed of reduced visibility?

A. No.

34. Q. Had you given any instructions to the officers of the deck about reporting or not reporting reduced visibility?

A. Yes. The captain's night order book includes that requirement in the instructions posted in the front of the book.

35. Q. If you had known that the visibility varied from one hundred yards to one thousand yards as testified by the other witnesses, would you have maintained the course you were on and the speed you were making?

A. Yes, because I felt that we were clear of all land and this course was the course to my area, which I wanted to reach at the earliest possible time.

36. Q. Had you determined the course that the submarine was to proceed on after charging?

A. The navigator had determined the course and I had checked the course and approved it. This course was two degrees to the left of the line from my position to the position at which I wished to dive at daylight.

37. Q. Why, in your night orders for this night, did you advise the officer of the deck, "Keep careful watch for land, breakers, or other indications of land, as we may be set toward shore"?

A. That is a precautionary instruction that is always given when as of a necessity lying to and charging our batteries with land in the vicinity and the lack of knowledge due to no past experience in these waters. -42-

38. Q. Knowing that you were in the vicinity of land, did you have an anchor ready for letting go?

A. The submerged anchor is always ready for letting go and can be released within thirty seconds from the time the order is given.

39. Q. When the ship was lying to charging, was any effort made to obtain a sounding by the hand lead?

A. No effort was made to obtain a sounding by use of the hand lead. This would involve placing a man on deck, which is not consistent with the condition of readiness of the vessel for diving at a moment's notice. I considered we were near enemy forces and felt that no time should be lost in submerging the boat if the presence of any vessel was indicated.

40. Q. Before departure from Dutch Harbor on this cruise, were efforts made to obtain reliable information from local sources regarding the dangers to be expected in the area where you were assigned?

A. All efforts to obtain information on the area to which I was going had been made from all sources known to me.

41. Q. What is your opinion as to the feasibility of salvage operations?

A. Salvage operations under the present war time conditions do not appear feasible to me. Salvage would require special vessels and equipment, which would be endangered by the known proximity of the enemy.

42. Q. What disposition was made of the torpedoes aboard the ship?

A. The torpedoes are all in the torpedo room forward. Four of them are in the torpedo tubes. The other eight are secured in the torpedo racks. The high pressure air in the eight torpedoes in the racks was bled off because of the resultant explosion and danger if any of them had been jarred loose due to the pounding, and punctured.

43. Q. Do you believe that the damage to the ship is becoming progressively worse?

A. I do. During my visits to the ship after the first day, the heavy pounding was still in progress, and on my last visit on the twenty-second the pounding had definitely broken loose framing and structure on the bottom of the ship. I believe that the first bad weather from the south or southeast will cause the ship to be broken beyond all possible salvage.

44. Q. Do you believe there is any possibility of recovering the torpedoes from the boat if it is decided to demolish her?

A. No, I do not. It would require a major operation because the torpedo room and battery room are flooded and the hatches are under water.

45. Q. Did you make any effort to get rid of the torpedoes before abandoning ship?

A. No effort was made to get rid of the torpedoes before abandoning ship because the pounding and rolling of the ship prevented the torpedo men from handling the torpedoes, and when decision was made to abandon, it was felt that they would be safer in the submarine than any other place. The four in the tubes were not expelled because of the danger involved to personnel. I felt that the ship might be pulled off and therefore did nothing to remove the torpedoes. When decision was made to abandon, the safety of personnel seemed to me paramount.   -45-

46. Q. The night order book says, "Call me when charge is completed". Was this order carried out?

A. The charge was never completed. However, I was informed when the charging on two engines had been completed and when the ship went ahead on one engine.

None of the parties to the investigation desired further to examine this witness.

The board informed the witness that he was privileged to make any further statement covering anything relating to the subject matter of the investigation which he thought should be a matter of record in connection therewith, which had not been fully brought out by the previous questioning.

The witness stated that he had nothing further to say.

The witness was duly warned and resumed his seat as defendant.

At this stage of the proceedings it becomes evident that O. M. Butler, Lieutenant, U. S. Navy, L. H. Young, Lieutenant junior grade, U. S. Naval Reserve, and T. E. Krueger, Boatswain, U. S. Navy, had become interested parties, and they were so designated. They were accordingly called before the board and informed of the gist of the testimony that seemed to implicate them, and informed of their rights. They examined the convening order and stated that they did not object to any member.

The interested parties waived the right to counsel. The provisions of Section 734(d), Naval Courts and Boards, were complied with.

Lieutenant Butler, an interested party, was called as a witness by the recorder and warned that his previous oath was still binding.

Examined by the board:

1. Q. State your name, rank, and present station;

A. Ovid McMaster Butler, Lieutenant, U. S. Navy, formerly engineer officer and communication officer of the U.S.S. S-27.

2. Q. Were you the officer of the deck and, if so, at what times on the evening of the eighteenth of June?

A. I was officer of the deck from the time we surfaced, which was shortly after seven o'clock, until a few minutes before nine o'clock.

3. Q. What was the state of the weather when you assumed the duties as officer of the deck?

A. There was a condition of light fog. I would estimate the visibility at about one to two miles.

4. Q. Was there a change in the state of the weather and, if so, what was the degree of change during your watch?

A. I would say there was no change other than the fact that it was beginning to get a little bit dark at nine o'clock, but not sufficient to reduce the visibility perceptibly.

5. Q. Did you make any weather reports to the commanding officer during your watch?

—44—

A. No, sir, I didn't.

6. Q. Why?

A. Because the commanding officer left the bridge at eight fifteen and between that time and the time I was relieved there was no change in the visibility conditions.

None of the parties to the investigation desired further to examine this witness.

The board informed the witness that he was privileged to make any further statement covering anything relating to the subject matter of the investigation which he thought should be a matter of record in connection therewith, which had not been fully brought out by the previous questioning.

The witness stated that he had nothing further to say.

The witness was duly warned and resumed his seat as an interested party.

Lieutenant junior grade L. H. Young, an interested party, was called as a witness by the recorder and warned that his previous oath was still binding.

Examined by the board:

1. Q. State your name, rank, and present duties.

A. Lawrence Hilgard Young, Lieutenant junior grade, U. S. Naval Reserve. I was communication officer, stores officer, educational officer, and sound officer on the S-27.

2. Q. Were you the officer on the deck between 2100 and 2400 on the evening of the eighteenth of June?

A. Yes, sir, I was.

3. Q. Tell the board what the state of the weather was and of any changes you observed during your watch.

A. When I came on to relieve Mr. Butler I would estimate visibility at two miles. You could not see the horizon but it was not raining and there was possibly a fog or mist near the horizon which blotted it from view. I did not feel that the visibility decreased to such an extent as to report it to the commanding officer. I recall looking through the binoculars trying to see the horizon but I could not see it. However, I felt that possibly it was clearing as it got darker, as the visibility seemed to me to be the same throughout the watch.

4. Q. What would you estimate the visibility during your watch?

A. I would say between one and a half and two miles by the horizon, but it was very hard to judge visibility.

5. Q. What entry had you made in the log concerning visibility?

A. I had made no entry in my log.

6. Q. No entries were made?

A. I myself made no entries.

7. Q. You are aware, are you not, that the visibility is entered in the log and that the officer of the deck signs the log, and this signature means the entry is correct?   -45-

A. Yes, sir, I am aware of that.

8. Q. Do you remember the entry in the log?

A. No, sir, I have not seen the log since that time, except watches at Amchitka which were signed by me.

9. Q. I show you the deck log. What entry of visibility is made during your watch?

A. It says here "One thousand yards".

10. Q. Is that a correct entry?

A. Well, that would be a half a mile. I am not sure that that is correct, sir.

11. Q. Do you care to restate your estimate of visibility?

A. I am trying to recall the picture from nine to twelve and I recall definitely there didn't seem to be a change warranting calling the commanding officer to the bridge. Apparently there was a large decrease just before we struck the reefs at Amchitka, because if the visibility was down to three hundred at that time, there must have been a great decrease in there, but I do not recall it having occurred during the nine to twelve watch.

12. Q. You have stated that the visibility at the time of grounding was three hundred yards. Is this an estimate by your own observation?

A. No, sir, that was based on the remark you made at the opening of the testimony -- the resume you gave when I was designated an interested party.

13. Q. Did you go on deck after the grounding?

A. Just a minute or so, sir, then I went below to arrange for food and mess gear, and so forth. I was calling orders down the hatch and I can't give an accurate estimate of the visibility at that time.

None of the parties to the investigation desired further to examine this witness.

The board informed the witness that he was privileged to make any further statement covering anything relating to the subject matter of the investigation which he thought should be a matter of record in connection therewith, which had not been fully brought out by the previous questioning.

The witness stated that he had nothing further to say.

The witness was duly warned and resumed his seat as an interested party.

At this stage of the proceedings it appeared to the board that Lieutenant O. M. Butler was no longer an interested party. He was so informed, and withdrew.

T. E. Krueger, Boatswain, U. S. Navy, an interested party, was recalled by the recorder and informed that his previous oath was still binding.

Examined by the board:

1. Q. You were the officer of the deck from midnight until the time of the grounding, were you not?

—46—

A. Yes, sir.

2. Q. Tell the board what the situation of the weather was when you came on watch and at the time of grounding, and any changes that were observed and, if so, what they were.

A. I agree with Lieutenant Young insofar as the state of the weather was, with the exception of the limits of visibility, which I think was about a half mile. There was no change in the visibility until just about the time that we sighted the land, at which time there was a mist that seemed to be setting along the coast. At this time I immediately called the captain and changed course to the left.

3. Q. Two lookouts have testified that they were unable to use their binoculars during the midwatch because the mist and foggy conditions rendered it impracticable. Can you comment on this?

A. At night when looking through binoculars there is not enough light to make visibility any clearer with a pair of binoculars. Another thing, in weather that we were encountering up there, it was practically impossible to keep the mist off the lens of the binoculars. They would cloud up as soon as we would wipe them off. We were moving at the time and the air being moist that way and hitting the binoculars would tend to cause them to fog up even more rapidly than when the ship was lying to.

4. Q. Where is the deck log kept in a submarine?

A. Down in the control room.

5. Q. Who makes the entries in the book?

A. Normally the quartermaster.

6. Q. Where is the quartermaster's station under way?

A. He is stationed on the bridge with the officer of the deck. He is the officer of the deck's assistant.

7. Q. Does he go below deck for entries?

A. He does at the end of the watch.

8. Q. He doesn't make hourly entries?

A. No, sir.

9. Q. Are any entries on the left hand page made when submerged?

A. No, sir, not as a rule.

10. Q. Is it possible to make the necessary observations?

A. Only one or two — condition of the clouds, possible wind direction but no force, the visibility, and the course on. As far as the barometer and the temperature is concerned, they are down in the boat and the pressure of the boat would render that useless.

None of the parties to the investigation desired further to examine this witness.

The board informed the witness that he was privileged to make any further statement covering anything relating to the subject matter of the investigation which he thought should be a matter of record in connection therewith, which had not been fully brought out by the previous questioning.

The witness stated that he had nothing further to say.   —47—

The witness was duly warned and resumed his seat as an interested party.

Neither the board, the recorder, nor any party to the investigation desired to call any more witnesses.

The investigation was finished, all parties thereto withdrawing.

-48-

After full and mature deliberation the board finds as follows:

FINDING OF FACTS

1. The S-27 grounded on the southeast coast of Amchitka Island, Aleutian Islands, in approximately latitude 51°22' north and longitude 179°36'30" east at 0043, June 19, 1942.

2. The S-27 was in diving trim with the conning tower hatch open, main and auxiliary inductions open, and water tight doors open.

3. The S-27 was under way, on the surface, swinging to the left from course 305°(T) to 225°(T) at a speed of six knots on the starboard engine, and grounded on a heading of about 285°(T).

4. The port engine was being used to charge batteries.

5. Land was sighted about one point on the starboard bow shortly before grounding.

6. Visibility was reduced by darkness and mist.

7. The officer of the deck changed course promptly to the left on sighting land in an attempt to avoid grounding.

8. The S-27 had been reconnoitering the east end of Amchitka Island and was proceeding to assigned patrol area in compliance with orders.

9. Collision quarters was sounded at about the time of grounding.

10. Shortly after grounding, all water tight doors were closed. Number three main ballast, forward and after trim tanks, forward and after fuel groups were blown dry. Number nine fuel tank was pumped out to 5,000 gallons. High pressure pump was started on motor and engine room bilges. Air pressure was put on motor room to check flooding from buckled bilge plates.

11. The proper chart as provided by the Navy Department was used in navigating.

12. The position of the ship was last determined by cross bearing on tangents of headlands on the southeastern end of Amchitka Island at 1735, June 18, 1942.

13. The courses steered and times of changing course were entered in the log book.

14. The speeds and distances made good are not entered in the log book.

15. The error of the gyro compass in use had not been determined for several days.

16. The magnetic compass was unreliable.

17. Leadsmen were not in the chains.

18. Anchors and chains were not ready for instant use.

19. The S-27 was not equipped with a fathometer or sounding machine. *-49-*

20. Lookouts were properly posted.

21. The sound equipment was not used for navigational purposes.

22. No soundings were taken with the hand lead.

23. The starboard shaft and propeller were rendered inoperative.

24. The draft before grounding was approximately seventeen feet six inches forward and twenty-one feet six inches aft.

25. The draft after grounding was approximately seventeen feet three inches forward and seventeen feet aft.

26. There was no list before or after grounding.

27. General distribution of variable weights before grounding was:

Forward trim tank	9,000 pounds.
Auxiliary tank	32,000 pounds.
Regulator tank	Dry.
After trim tank	Full of fresh water, 11,600 lbs.
Number three main ballast	5,000 gallons diesel, 4,000 gallons salt water.
Battery water tank	550 gallons.
Fresh water tank	1,000 gallons.
Forward fuel group	4,214 gallons.
After fuel group	5,313 gallons.
Number nine fuel oil tank	8,171 gallons.
Main lub oil tank	780 gallons.
Reserve lub oil tank	1,500 gallons.
Main drain	Flooded.

Provisions in normal stowage.
Four torpedoes in tubes - not flooded.
Eight torpedoes in racks.

28. Pounding against the rocks caused progressive flooding of compartments in the following order:
Auxiliary tank.
Number one and number two main ballast tanks.
Torpedo room.
Forward battery room.

29. When last observed the torpedo room was completely flooded.

30. There is no evidence of unsatisfactory performance of any water tight appliance or fitting.

31. Radio aids to navigation were not available.

32. Records of times and bearings taken of terrestial objects were properly kept.

33. No ship's positions were recorded in the log book for June 17, 1942.

34. The 0800 and 2000 ship's positions were not recorded in the log book for June 18, 1942.

35. The commanding officer was not on the bridge from 2015 to the time of grounding.

36. The navigator did not go on the bridge from time of surfacing at 1920 until the time of grounding.   -5a-

37. There was no loss of life nor injury to personnel.

38. No material or equipage of any consequence was salvaged.

-51-

OPINION

1. The set and drift of the tidal currents in this area cannot be accurately pre-determined.

2. The times of high and low water in this area cannot be accurately determined from existing publications.

3. The S-27 drifted into a dangerous position during the period from 2005 to 0027 while she was lying to charging batteries.

4. The S-27 is a total loss and salvage operations are not practicable for the following reasons:

    (1) Special equipment would be required and is not immediately available.
    (2) Salvage operations would be prolonged.
    (3) The S-27 will probably break up before salvage can be completed.
    (4) The proximity of the enemy.
    (5) The coast at the point of grounding is unsheltered and poorly charted.
    (6) Prevalent unfavorable weather.

5. The commanding officer, Lieutenant Commander Herbert L. Jukes, U.S. Navy, is responsible for the grounding because a course, unsafe under the visibility conditions that existed, was set in close proximity to an unfamiliar, unlighted, poorly charted coast, without due consideration to the unknown direction and strength of currents and tidal streams.

6. The navigator, Lieutenant Frank McElhany Smith, U.S. Navy, is also responsible for the grounding of the S-27 in that he failed to employ all the means at his disposal to fix the position of the ship, and because he did not realise the dangerous position of the ship and so advise the commanding officer as was his duty to do so.

    The officer of the deck, T. E. Krueger, Boatswain, U.S. Navy, is responsible for the grounding to a lesser degree in that he proceeded and continued on a prescribed course at two thirds speed on one engine under increasingly poor visibility and failed to inform his commanding officer of these conditions.

CHARLES C. PULEGER,
Commander, U.S. Navy.

THOMAS C. THOMAS,
Lieutenant Commander, U.S. Navy.

JAY S. ANDERSON,
Lieutenant Commander, U.S. Navy.

The record of proceedings of the third day of the investigation was read and approved, the board being cleared during the reading of so much thereof as pertains to the proceedings in cleared court, and the board having finished the investigation, then, at 7:00 p.m., July 5, 1942, adjourned to await the action of the convening authority.

CHARLES C. PFLEGER,
Commander, U.S. Navy,
Senior Member.

JAY S. ANDERSON,
Lieutenant Commander, U.S. Navy,
Recorder

-53-

SS132/L11-1/A4-1   U.S.S. S-27

Serial   June 29, 1942

From: The Commanding Officer.
To :   The Commander-in-Chief, U.S. Fleet.
Via :   (1) The Commander Submarine Division Forty One.
               (2) The Commander Submarine Squadron Four.
               (3) The Commander Submarines, Pacific Fleet.
               (4) The Commander-in-Chief, Pacific Fleet.

Subject: U.S.S. S-27 (SS132) - Grounding and Subsequent Loss of.

Reference: (a) Article 840 U.S. Navy Regulations.

Enclosure: (A) Narrative of events prior to the grounding and
                   subsequent loss of the U.S.S. S-27 and the events
                   immediately afterwards.

       1.   In compliance with reference (a), it is reported that
the U.S.S. S-27 was grounded and lost on June 19, 1942.

       2.   Enclosure (A), setting forth the circumstances is for-
warded herewith.

       3.   Article 841(3) U.S. Navy Regulations has been complied
with by an identical report forwarded direct to the Secretary of the Navy.

                                    H. L. JUKES

                        "A"(1)

ENCLOSURE "A"

The following is a narrative of the events prior to the grounding and subsequent loss of the U.S.S. S-27 and the events immediately afterwards.

After surfacing on the night of 16 June 1942, we received a message directing us to leave our patrol area off of KULUK BAY and proceed to assigned area at KISKA ISLAND via AMCHITKA PASS. Prior to leaving DUTCH HARBOR for patrol I had received verbal orders from the Division Commander to inspect CONSTANTINE HARBOR, AMCHITKA ISLAND for the presence of enemy activity.

The course was set to clear to the northward of the islands by five miles and the distance to travel indicated our arrival off CONSTANTINE HARBOR about 0100 (plus 12) on the 18th of June. We were able to obtain fixes until we rounded GARELOI ISLAND and headed across AMCHITKA PASS on course 245°T. At 2245 I went to the bridge to see if AMCHITKA ISLAND had been sighted and to be present if a landfall was made. At 2400 when nothing could be seen ahead I changed course to 270°T, in order to make certain of landfall in case the current, (of which I had no information) had set us to the south and east during the passage. After steaming for one hour at two thirds speed (8 knots) on this course 270°T, without sighting anything the decision was made to circle with 10° rudder until light conditions were better. I was concerned about being able to see land because the Coast Pilot and the Confidential Chart showed that the entire island was low and we might not have been able to see it in time to prevent grounding. This was done even knowing that the 0100 D.R. position still gave me 7½ miles of open water.

At 0204 steadied on course 090°T. and dived at 0207. From that time until 0556 we steered various courses until I picked up the island and obtained a fix. There after we patrolled until 1300 when I decided that I should leave if I wanted to get around the southern end before time to surface and charge batteries. It was deemed advisable to stay submerged during daylight because the enemy was known to be within 70 miles and I had no report of their air activities.

The decision to round the island to the southward was based upon the following factors:

1. Previous reports received indicated the presence of the enemy on SEMISOPOCHNOI ISLAND. Therefore, knowing they were at KISKA ISLAND, it seemed likely that there might be air patrols between the two. A northern route for me might disclose my presence and I wanted to reach my area (090°T. to 120°T. from north head KISKA HARBOR) undetected if possible.

2. To have entered my area from the north would have hemmed me in by RAT ISLAND, LITTLE SITKIN ISLAND and subsequently the unknown currents of KISKA PASS and RAT ISLAND PASS where little enemy surface shipping might be expected, whereas a southern approach left me free water to the north for movement and retirement if necessary.

3. I had decided to run my patrol on a northwest - southeast line five to ten miles southwest of RAT ISLAND and TANADAK PASS retiring at night to the south, or southeast to charge batteries. Consequently, the southern approach, rounding AMCHITKA to the south, seemed to me the most logical route.

After rounding EAST CAPE on AMCHITKA ISLAND at 1330 numerous tangential fixes were obtained and a set to the north of about two knots was determined. Currents of this magnitude are known to exist and had been previously encountered in other ALEUTIAN ISLAND PASSES. Consequently, at 1735 speed was increased to 6 knots and course adjusted in order to permit rounding ST. MAKARIUS PT. and being at least five miles from the island prior to 2000 when it would be necessary to surface and lie to for a charge for a period of at least four hours. I felt that this position would remove me from the influence of the currents in the PASS. No information on currents to be encountered in my area was available.

At 1920 the ship was surfaced, visibility from 2 - 3 miles, and the island was not in sight because of a fog bank.

In order to close the line which I had decided to steer for my area I went ahead at 1929 on course 315°T. at a speed of 8 knots and stopped at 2005 in order to start the battery charge. The D.R. position at this time placed the ship 6 miles west of ST. MAKARIUS PT. It had been my policy to lie to and charge about 5-6 miles off of any land available. I felt that this position provided the least chance of detection either by RADAR or VISUAL search because of our blending with the shore background.

At 2010 the charge was started and at 2015 I was relieved of the deck by the O.O.D. Conditions at this time were: Visibility 2-3 miles, calm sea, sky overcast and the island not in sight. I instructed the O.O.D. and lookouts to be especially on the alert for land.

At 2030 the oncoming O.O.D. for the 2100 to 0000 watch was given the same instructions by me as to alertness for land.

At 2200 the night order book was written and made available for the O.O.D. In the night order book instructions were given to set course 305°T. speed 5 knots when one engine was released from charging, to keep a careful watch for land, and if in doubt as to position as regards proximity to beach to change course to 225°T. and to call me.

At 0027 the O.O.D. went ahead six knots on starboard engine and came left from 050°T. (upon which head the vessel lay to) to 305°T. as per instructions, and informed me. At about 0043 the O.O.D. reported he was coming left to 225°T. with full left rudder as he thought he had sighted land on the starboard bow. I immediately started for the bridge and simultaneously the ship struck.

The sequence of events that immediately preceded the grounding, as reported by the O.O.D. Boatswain T. E. Krueger, U.S. Navy, are as follows:

"A dark object believed to be land, suddenly loomed up about one point on the starboard bow and was sighted simultaneously by the O.O.D., quartermaster and starboard lookout. The O.O.D. ordered "left full rudder, come to course 225°T. and report to the captain that I think I have sighted land on the starboard bow and am changing course to 225°T." Almost immediately thereafter the O.O.D. saw small breakers about 25 yards forward of the bow and rang up "back emergency", on both engines order telegraphs and sounded the collision alarm. The ship struck almost immediately thereafter."

I arrived on the bridge at this time. The port motor was backing and the starboard started backing within a few seconds and the ship was reported rigged for collision. The ship was bumping violently on the rocks and rolling about 10° to 15° on each side. The motors were continued at back emergency until it was seen that the vessel was held from going astern by a submerged rock. Orders were then given to blow the fuel from the No. 3 Main Ballast Tank, the after fuel group and all variable tanks. Efforts were continued to back clear as the vessel became lighter during which time a tendency for the stern to swing to starboard against rocks was established, and the starboard screw struck and was disabled. It was necessary to force the ship ahead in order to clear the stern. During this period it was found that the ship could be moved only about 20 feet forward or aft before it became held fast. Attempts were continued until all tanks were blown dry with the exception of a small amount of fuel amidships.

After these attempts to clear by backing and filling had failed the area was sounded for possible passage through which the vessel might be warped but none was found.   "A"(3)

At 0115 the first message was encoded and broadcast. In all, five were sent. They appear at the end of this narrative.

At 0330 plans were made to remove the greater part of the crew because the pounding was increasing and I felt that the tanks might give at any moment resulting in danger to the crew that could be avoided. The rubber life boat was brought up on deck and made ready. One officer and one man, both capable swimmers, were first sent in to the beach and reported back that conditions were favorable once the boat cleared the first rocks close to the ship. A "ferry" system was then used with lines to the boat and the beach. Provisions, dry and warm clothing, guns, medical supplies and men were safely transferred. By about 1100 all but five men and myself were landed. By this time the breakers had increased so that further trips for provisions were not safe.

Prior to leaving the ship the following equipment which I considered might prove advantageous to the enemy if discovered was completely destroyed:

1. ECM:- all wheels broken and scattered in deep water. Type-writer part destroyed by hammer and thrown in deep water. Nothing remains in ship but the safe which is empty.

2. QC - JK equipment demolished with hammer. QC head was run out when vessel grounded.

3. JK in torpedo room demolished.

4. Mk 3 Torpedo Angle solver thrown overboard as far as possible seaward.

5. All torpedo approach data and tables burned.

6. All confidential and secret publications, codes, ciphers and crypto aids were taken ashore and burned. Unburnable confidential items were broken and thrown in deep water.

At 1530 three of the remaining men were gotten ashore. At this time the heavy pounding had definitely loosened the side plating for it could be heard rattling at each jar of the ship. The torpedo room was slowly flooding although an air pressure had been built up in this compartment. An angle of six degrees down by the head was noticed. The propellers were clear of the water.

At 1550 as nothing could be done further to help the ship, and the torpedo room was about one half flooded, I decided to leave. The remaining compartments were made watertight and the radioman, second officer and myself went ashore.

Crew and provisions had been landed in an unsheltered cove, the surface of which was covered with rocks and small boulders. Fires had been started and wet clothing removed. No injuries were reported and aside from being exhausted the crew was in very good condition. Each man was given about 1½ ounces of pure alcohol in hot coffee. Fires were going all night but because of the very cold wind and rain no rest was obtained.

At 0430 on the 20th, of June all hands except 10 started out to search for Constantine Harbor. The inspection by periscope on the previous day disclosed a church and a few small buildings there. By 0900 all had arrived at the deserted village. The buildings proved adequate for the entire crew. Coal, diesel oil and gasoline were available and stoves rigged in three buildings.

"A" (4)

On the following day camp routine was established, fourteen camp orders published, armed sentries and lookouts were posted and a regular routine was put into effect. This was done in order to provide something for the men to do and to prevent any attempts at slackness in discipline. The entire crew responded admirably throughout this entire period and it was noted that each man tried to pull even more than his own weight.

The next three days were spent in trips to the cove for supplies. The ship was boarded on the 21st. and 22nd. by me and a volunteer party, and more provisions landed. Trips to the ship were only possible during early morning. Conditions aboard were becoming worse. On the 21st. I boarded and found the forward battery compartment beginning to flood. Chlorine gas was present as no further attempts were made to enter this compartment. The control room bilges were about 2/3 filled. Other compartments dry. Landing on board was becoming difficult due to the increased down angle which allowed the seas to break over the only place available to land. On the last trip the hatches were closed and no further trips were attempted.

Provisions obtained could last for about 30 days by rationing. This was started on the first day ashore for I had no knowledge as to whether my last two messages had been received and I also felt that our nearness to the enemy might prevent rescue until some late date.

On 24 June a PBY plane circled and landed. The pilot had been on a routine flight and fortunately passed over the Harbor. Fifteen of the crew were rescued. On 25 June three planes removed the remainder of the crew.

All guns salvaged from the ship were destroyed. Nothing of value remains at Constantine Harbor except canned provisions, blankets and winter clothing.

H. L. JUKES

"A"(5)

APPENDIX TO NARRATIVE

COPIES OF MESSAGES SENT AND RECEIVED ON 19 JUNE 1942:

MESSAGES SENT

1. AGROUND PENDING SOUTHEAST SIDE AMCHITKA ISLAND.

   TIME - 0110 (plus 12)
   ADDRESSED TO ANY OR ALL U.S. SHIPS.
   FREQUENCIES USED: 8270, 12705, 4305.
   AIRCRAFT CODE USED.

2. TIN CAN GET IN OFF SCREWS DISABLED.

   TIME - 0145
   ADDRESSED TO - ANY OR ALL U.S. NAVY SHIPS.
   FREQUENCIES: 8270, 12705, 4305, 2190.
   AIRCRAFT CODE USED.

3. IMPROPERLY CODED.

   SENT AT 0440 (plus 12)

4. CANCEL MY NINETEEN SIXTEEN FORTY X USSCRO SQUARLY ST. MAKARIUS
   REPEAT ST. MAKARIUS POINT AMCHITKA X PORT SCREW WORKING ON WATER
   BUT MOTOR ROOM EXPECTED TO FLOOD ANY TIME X UNABLE TO BACK OVER
   ROCKS X BELIEVE CAN BE PULLED CLEAR BY TUG X ALL TANKS DRY X
   POUNDING IS BAD X AM PREPARED TO ABANDON X HEAVY FOG.

   SENT TO CSD41, INFO CTF 8.
   FREQUENCIES USED: 8270, 12705, 4305, CSP 1037(A) AND 1038(A) USED.

5. HEAVY POUNDING CONTINUES X ENDLESS X BRAMS GONE IN BALLAST TANKS X
   ALL ASHORE EXCEPT SIX X ALL COMPARTMENT DRY BUT TORPEDO ROOM X WILL
   STAY UNTIL UNTENABLE X CRYPTO AIDS DESTROYED BUT THIS X WHEN
   ABANDONED WILL TAKE CREW TO CONSTANTINE HARBOR THIS FREE OF ENEMY
   ON EIGHTEENTH

   SENT TO CSD41, CTF8, INFO. COMALSEC. CSP 1037(A) USED.
   FREQUENCY: 8270, TIME 1245 (plus 12)

6. DUE SEA CONDITIONS AM ABANDONING SHIP X IF POSSIBLE WILL RETURN
   TOMORROW OTHERWISE CONSTANTINE MY TWENTY ZERO ONE FORTY FIVE.

   TO CSD41, CTF8, INFO. COMALSEC.
   TIME: 1513 (plus 12)
   FREQ. 8270
   CODE: CSP 1037(A) 1038(A)

MESSAGES RECEIVED

1. WHAT IS YOUR POSITION X USE SECRET CRYPTO CHANNEL X AMPLIFY REPORT
   OF SCREWS DISABLED.

   FROM CTG 8.6
   TIME: 0530 (plus 12)

2. MY NINETEEN SEVENTEEN THIRTY REQUESTED POSITION AND DETAILS SAIL
   TWENTY SEVEN X ESTIMATED POSITION VICINITY AMCHITKA ISLAND.

   FROM: CSD41
   TO : COMALSEC
   INFO: S-27
   TIME: 0754 (plus 12)

"A" (6)

3.   WHAT IS YOUR POSITION ANSWER SECURE CYPHER IF NOT IN TROUBLE.

FROM: ANY OR ALL U.S. SHIPS
TO :   S-27
TIME: 0849 (plus 12)

"A" (7)

UNITED STATES SHIP _____ S-27 _____ Thurs _____ 18 _____ June _____, 19__

ZONE DESCRIPTION + 12 _____   **REMARKS**

0-4   Underway on course 245° T+G 260° T, making 2/3 speed ahead on all engines, enroute ADAK
ISLAND to AMCHITKA ISLAND, ALEUTIAN ISLANDS 0001 c/c to 270° T+G 285° PSC ___ 0__
started circling to starboard with 10° rudder. 0204 steadied on course 090° T+G 093° PSC
090° T. Made quick dive on course 090° T. 0305 c/c to 130° T+G, 150° PSC.   0341 c/s +_
215° T+G 260° PSC.

                                                    (s) O. M. Butler

4-8   Underway as before. 0604 Sighted AMCHITKA ISLAND bearing 177° T, distance abt 10 miles.
0305 c/c to 180° T+G 179° PSC. 0606 c/c to 236° T+G 255° PSC. 0644 c/c to 312° T+G
312° PSC. 0740 c/c to 110° T+G.

                                                    (s) L. B. Young

8-12 Underway as before. 0840 c/c to 300° T+G 312° PSC. 0902 c/c to 250° T+G 243° PSC.
1024 c/c to 273° T+G 300 PSC. 1028 c/c to 230° T+G 240° PSC. 1032 Started circling
to right. 1041 Steadied on course 090° T+G 095° PSC. 1055 c/c to 330° T+G 325° PSC.
1100 c/c to 030° T+G 016° PSC. 1113 Started circling to the right. 1115 Steadied on
course 090° T+G 095° PSC. 1118 Sighted plane on parallel course, altitude 500 feet,
distance 3/4 mile flying toward us. Made daily inspection of magazines and sampled
powder samples, conditions normal.

                                                    (s) F. M. Smith

12-16 Underway as before. 1220 c/c to 120° T+G 090° PSC. 1315 c/c to 180° T+G 165° PSC.
1340 c/c to 230° T+G 255° PSC. 1435 c/c to 272° T+G 300° PSC. 1530 c/c to 245 T+G
260° T. 1655 c/c to 265° T+G 290° PSC.

                                                    (s) C. R. Krueger

16-20 Underway as before. 1707 c/c to 240° T+G 265° PSC. 1736 c/c to 270° T+G 325 PSC.
1738 c/c to 180° T+G 144° PSC. 1805 c/c to 240° T+G 267° PSC. 1_3 c/c to 180° T+G.
1915 c/c to 210° T+G 220° PSC. 1920 Surfaced and c/s to 315° T 717 PS, and went ahead
2/3 speed on all engines.

                                                    (s) O. M. Butler

20-24 Underway as before. 2000 Stopped all engines. 2010 Started charging main storage
batteries on all engines.

                                                    (s) L. B. Young

Approved: Examined:

                                                    (s) F. M. Smith

(s) I. L. Jukes   Lt. U. S. N., Navigator.

LOG OF THE UNITED STATES SHIP __S-27__ (Name)   __SS 132__ (Identification Number)

AT PASSAGE __Amchitka Island A.I.__ TO __Kiska I. A.I.__ , __Fri__ (Day) __12__ (Date) __June__ (Month) 19__42__

ZONE DESCRIPTION __+12__   __H. L. Jukes__   Lieut.__U. S. Navy, Commanding.__

Time	"ALL PURPOSE" AVERAGE REVOLUTIONS	BY REVS.		BY LOG		COURSE (P. C.) Gyro___ Mag.___ (indicate which)	WIND		BAROMETER		TEMPERATURE			WEATHER, BY SYMBOLS	CLOUDS				SEA	
		NAUTICAL MILES	TENTHS	NAUTICAL MILES	TENTHS		DIRECTION	FORCE	HEIGHT IN INCHES	READING AT ATTACHED A. THER.	AIR, DRY BULB	AIR, WET BULB	WATER AT SURFACE		FORM	MOVING FROM—	AMOUNT	VISIBILITY	DIRECTION	STATE OF SURFACE
	1	2	3	4	5	6	7	8	9	10	11	12	13	14	15	16	17	18	19	20
A.M.																				
1	272	2	0			280	S	0	2990		42		42	F	--	S	10	0.3	1	S
2						280	S	1	2990		42			F		S	10	0.4	1	S
3						280	S	1	2989		42			F		S	10	0.5	1	S
4						280	S	1	2988		42			F		S	10	0.5	1	S
5						280	S	1	2988		43			F		S	10	0.5	1	S
6						280	S	1	2989		43			F		S	10	1	1	S
7						280	S	1	2990		43			F		S	10	1	1	S
8						280	S	1	2990		43			F		S	10	1	1	S
9						280	S	1	2992		43			F		S	10	1	1	S
10						280	S	1	2993		44			F		S	10	2	1	S
11						280	S	1	2991		44			F		S	10	2	1	S
12						280	S	1	2990		44			F		S	10	2	1	S

(Latitude / Longitude section)			**DRILLS AND EXERCISES**	
⦿ Latitude_____	Port { Received_____			
⦿ Longitude_____	{ Expended_____		*Morning*	*Afternoon*
	{ On hand_____	Division		
⦿ Latitude_____		1_____		
⦿ Longitude_____	Water { Distilled_____	2_____		
	{ Received_____	3_____		
⦿ Latitude_____	{ Expended_____	4_____		
⦿ Longitude_____	{ On hand_____	5_____		
		6_____		
Current { Set_____	BEFORE LEAVING PORT	7_____		
{ Drift_____	Draft for'd_____	8_____		
	Draft aft_____	9_____		
GYROCOMPASS IN USE				
Error_____	AFTER ENTERING PORT			
	Draft for'd_____			
STANDARD MAG. COMPASS	Draft aft_____			
Compass No._____				
S. H._____	MAGAZINE TEMPERATURES:			
Error_____	Maximum_____			
Variation_____	Minimum_____			
Deviation_____				

Time						COURSE	WIND		BAROMETER		TEMP			WEATHER		CLOUDS				SEA
P.M.																				
13						280	S	1	2990		44			F		S	10	2	1	S
14						280	S	1	2987		44			F		S	10	2	1	S
15						280	S	1	2986		44			F		S	10	2	1	S
16						280	S	1	2985		44			F		S	10	2	1	S
17						280	S	1	2985		43			F		S	10	2		
18							S	1	2986		43			F		S	10	2		
19							S	1	2986		43			F		S	10	2		
20							S	1	2986		42			F		S	10	2		
21							S	1	2984		42			F		S	10	2		
22							S	1	2984		42			F		S	10	2		
23							S	1	2984		42			F		S	10	2		
24							S	1	2984		42			F		S	10	2		

SUBMERGED RUN DATA—SUBMARINES

	1	2	3	4	5
Run No. (Serial)					
Time to submerge					
Greatest depth					

LOG OF THE UNITED STATES SHIP _____ S-27 _____ (Name) _____ SS 132 _____ (Identification Number)

AT PASSAGE _____ Adak Island _____ TO _____ Amchitka Island Alaska _____, Thurs 18 June 1942
(Day) (Date) (Month)

ZONE DESCRIPTION +12 _____ H. L. Jukes _____, Lieut. U. S. Navy, Commanding.

Hour	"All Day?" Average Engine Revs	BY REVS.			BY LOG		Compass (P.C.)	WIND			BAROMETER	TEMPERATURE			Weather by Symbol	CLOUDS				SEA	
		Nautical Miles	Tenths	Nautical Miles	Tenths	Gyro / Mag (indicate which)	Direction	Force	Height in Inches	Reading at Ther.	Air, Dry Bulb	Air, Wet Bulb	Water at Surface		Form	Moving From—	Amount	Visibility	Direction	Cells / Force
	1	2	3	4	5	6	7	8	9	10	11	12	13	14	15	16	17	18	19	20
1						215	W	2	2992		43	43		OC	ST CU	W	10	10	3	NW
2						215	W	3	2992		42	43		OC	ST CU	W	10	10	2	NW
3																				
4																				
5																				
6																				
7									Submerged											
8																				
9																				
10																				
11																				
12																				

Latitude _____
Longitude _____

Latitude _____ N
Longitude _____ E

Latitude _____
Longitude _____

Current { Set _____ Drift _____

GYROCOMPASS IN USE

Error _____

STANDARD MAG. COMPASS

Compass No. _____
S. H. _____
Error _____
Variation _____
Deviation _____

Fuel { Received _____ Expended _____ On hand _____

Water { Distilled _____ Received _____ Expended _____ On hand _____

BEFORE LEAVING PORT
Draft for'd _____
Draft aft. _____

AFTER ENTERING PORT
Draft for'd _____
Draft aft. _____

MAGAZINE TEMPERATURES:
Maximum _____
Minimum _____

DRILLS AND EXERCISES

Drills	Morning	Afternoon
1		
2		
3		
4		
5		
6		
7		
8		
9		

Hour							Compass	Direction	Force	Barometer	Air Dry	Water	Weather		Form	Amount	Visibility	Direction	Force
13																			
14																			
15																			
16																			
17																			
18								Submerged											
19																			
20					315	W	2	2998	42	43	P	—	—	10	1.0	1	NW
21							2995	42	43	P	—	—	10	1.0	1	NW
22	Lying to			315	W	2	2994	42	43	P	—	—	10	1.0	1	NW
23				315	W	2	2991	42	43	P	—	—	10	1.0	1	NW
24				315	W	2	2990	42	43	P	—	—	0	1.0	1	NW

SUBMERGED RUN DATA—SUBMARINES

	1	2	3	4	5
Run No. (Serial)	8521				
Time to submerge	1.0 158				
Greatest depth	70"				

UNITED STATES SHIP _____ , 19 ___

(Day)   (Date)   (Month)

ZONE DESCRIPTION _____   **REMARKS**

Approved: Examined: "Exhibit 2" (1)

U. S. S. Navigator

UNITED STATES SHIP ___S-27___   **Fri** (Day)   **19** (Date)   **June** (Month) , 19⁴²

ZONE DESCRIPTION __+ 12__   **REMARKS**

0-4
This entry is now cancelled out.
Lying to off Amchitka Island, Alaska, charging main storage batteries on all engines. 0025 Secured charging main storage batteries on starboard engine. 0027 2/3 ahead on starboard engine, 270 rpm, 6 knots. Steadied on course 305° T-G 308° PSC. 0043 sighted dark outline on starboard bow, left full rudder to 225° T-G and went aground before clutches could be disengaged. Collision alarm was sounded and ship was rigged for collision. Tried backing on port motor but ship was apparently resting in cradle between two ridges of rock. Ship began pounding on the rocks as swells would roll in.

0-4
Lying to off Amchitka Is., A.Is., charging main storage batteries using both engines. 0020 Stopped sttd. engine; continued charge with the port engine. 0027 Sttd. engine ahead 2/3 spd., 270 rpm., 6 knots. Set course 305 true and gyro. 0035 Began charging main air banks with sttd. air compressor. About 0043 sighted land about 1 point off the sttd. bow about 1/4 of a mile or less. c/c to 225 true and gyro with full left rudder. About 0043½ sighted small breakers about 25 yds. fwd. of the bow. All motors back emergency. Sounded collision alarm. About 0043½ ship hit heavily on reef. About 0043-3/4 Captain arrived on the bridge. Rudder amidships. About 0044 All stop. About 0049 All motors back full spd. About 0046 All stop. About 0046 All motors back emergency. About 0051 All stop. About 0052 All motors ahd. full spd.; right full rudder. About 0054 Stopped port motor; sttd. mtr. ahead 2/3 spd. About 0055 All motors ahd. 2/3 spd. 0057 Sttd. mtr. stop, port motor back 1/3. 0058 Port motor back full spd. 0059 Port motor back emergency. 0100 Port motor back 1/3 spd. 0101 Stopped port motor. From 0101 to 0400 continued maneuvering at various speeds on both motors trying to work ship clear of reef.

(s) T. B. Krueger

4-8
Stranded as before. 0450 Landed first load of salvaged provisions with one officer and one man on Amchitka Island. Rubber lifeboat in use for salvage purposes. 0510 Commenced regular trips landing men and provisions. Auxiliary tank determined to be flooded to considerable extent. Leaks suspected in #1 and #2 main ballast tanks by air leaks alongside. Bilge plating in motor room pounded in considerably.

(s) F. W. Smith

8-12
Stranded as before. 0800 Ens. L. H. Young, USN, proceeded with party of 5 men to locate constanting harbor. Continued shifting men, provisions, clothing, firearms, and ammunition ashore. Proceeding with destruction of material and publications of confidential nature. Ship pounding very heavily with increasing seas.

(s) J. L. Smith

12-16
Stranded as before. 1200 Discontinued landing of material due to heaviness of seas and pounding of boat. Completed landing of all but Captain and 5 men. Completed destruction of confidential material and papers except such as landed by Communication Officer for possible use. 1400 Torpedo room determined to be flooding. 1430 Ship pounding extremely heavy on rocks and seas breaking over. Captain, one officer and four men abandoned ship. Established camp on Amchitka Island in a cove about one mile east of St. Makarius Point. Officers and crew ashore and no injuries received. Camp afforded no shelter and was very wet due to rains and mist. Records & accounts intact except T. B. Krueger, Bos'n, USN, (Temporary).

(s) F. W. Smith

16-20
Encamped as before.

(s) F. W. Smith

20-24
Encamped as before. 2030 Party which left at 0800 returned, two men having strayed from party at 1000 and not located.

(s) F. W. Smith

Exhibit I (3)

Approved: Examined:

(s) E. L. Jukes   (s) F. W. Smith

Lt. U.S.N., Navigator.

LOG OF THE UNITED STATES SHIP_____
(Name)   (Identification Number)

AT
PASSAGE _____ TO _____ , 19___
(Day)   (Date)   (Month)

ZONE DESCRIPTION _____ _____ U. S. Navy, Commanding.

Hour	"ALL SHIPS" AVERAGE REVOLUTIONS	BY REVS.		BY LOG		COURSE (P. C.)	WIND		BAROMETER		TEMPERATURE			WEATHER, BY SYMBOLS	CLOUDS				SEA	
		Nautical Miles	Tenths	Nautical Miles	Tenths	Gyro Mag. (Indicate which)	Direction	Force	Height in Inches	Reading at Ther.	Air, Dry Bulb	Air, Wet Bulb	Water at Surface		Form	Moving From—	Amount	Visibility	Direction	Scale (Force)
	1	2	3	4	5	6	7	8	9	10	11	12	13	14	15	16	17	18	19	20
A.M.																				
1																				
2																				
3																				
4																				
5																				
6																				
7																				
8																				
9																				
10																				
11																				
12																				

Latitude _____
Longitude _____

Latitude _____
Longitude _____

Latitude _____
Longitude _____

Current { Set _____
{ Drift _____

GYROCOMPASS IN USE
Error _____

STANDARD MAG. COMPASS
Compass No. _____
P. H. _____
Error _____
Variation _____
Deviation _____

Fuel { Received _____
{ Expended _____
{ On hand _____

Water { Distilled _____
{ Received _____
{ Expended _____
{ On hand _____

BEFORE LEAVING PORT
Draft for'd _____
Draft aft _____

AFTER ENTERING PORT
Draft for'd _____
Draft aft _____

MAGAZINE TEMPERATURES:
Maximum _____
Minimum _____

DRILLS AND EXERCISES

Division	Morning	Afternoon
1		
2		
3		
4		
5		
6		
7		
8		
9		

P.M.																				
1																				
2																				
3																				
4																				
5																				
6																				
7																				
8																				
9																				
10																				
11																				
12																				

SUBMERGED RUN DATA—SUBMARINES

	1	2	3	4	5
Run No. (Serial)					
Time to submerge					
Greatest depth					

LOG OF THE UNITED STATES SHIP_____
(Name)   (Identification Number)

AT
PASSAGE_____ TO_____, _____ ____ 19___
(Day)   (Time)   (Month)

ZONE DESCRIPTION_____   _____ U. S. Navy, Commanding.

HOUR	"ALL-SHIPS" AFTER (16 EXPIRED HOUR)	BY REVS.		BY LOG		COURSE (P.C.)	WIND		BAROMETER		TEMPERATURE			WEATHER, BY SYMBOLS	CLOUDS				SEA	
		NAUTICAL MILES	TURNS	NAUTICAL MILES	TENTHS	Gyro___ Mag.___ (Indicate which)	DIRECTION	FORCE	HEIGHT IN INCHES	READING AT. TEMP.	AIR, DRY BULB	AIR, WET BULB	WATER AT SURFACE		FORM	MOVING FROM—	AMOUNT	VISIBILITY	CONDITION	SWELL FROM—
	1	2	3	4	5	6	7	8	9	10	11	12	13	14	15	16	17	18	19	20
A.M.																				
1																				
2																				
3																				
4																				
5																				
6																				
7																				
8																				
9																				
10																				
11																				
12																				

Latitude_____
Longitude_____

Latitude_____
Longitude_____

Latitude_____
Longitude_____

Current { Set_____
          Drift_____

GYROCOMPASS IN USE

Error_____

STANDARD MAG. COMPASS

Compass No._____
S. H._____
Error_____
Variation_____
Deviation_____

Fuel { Received_____
       Expended_____
       On hand_____

Water { Distilled_____
        Received_____
        Expended_____
        On hand_____

BEFORE LEAVING PORT
Draft for'd_____
Draft aft_____

AFTER ENTERING PORT
Draft for'd_____
Draft aft_____

MAGAZINE TEMPERATURES:
Maximum_____
Minimum_____

DRILLS AND EXERCISES

Division	Morning	Afternoon
1		
2		
3		
4		
5		
6		
7		
8		
9		

HOUR																				
P.M.																				
13																				
14																				
15																				
16																				
17																				
18																				
19																				
20																				
21																				
22																				
23																				
24																				

SUBMERGED RUN DATA—SUBMARINES

	1	2	3	4	5
Run No. (Serial)					
Time to submerge					
Greatest depth					

"EXHIBIT 4"

July 1, 1942

From: Lieut. H. F. Nicholson, U.S. Navy.
To :   The Senior Member, Board of Investigation
         Concerning Grounding of U.S.S. S-27.

Subject: Navigation and position of U.S.S. S-27
          prior to and at moment of grounding.

References: (a) Naval Courts and Boards, Section 735.
             (b) Quartermaster's Notebook, U.S.S. S-27, for period
                 June 15 - June 19, 1942.
             (c) Confidential Chart No. 5640.
             (d) Ship's Bearing Book, U.S.S. S-27.

1. In accordance with reference (a), and upon receipt of verbal
orders from Senior Member, Board of Investigation Concerning Grounding of
U.S.S. S-27, the originating officer assumed the duties of Board Navigator
on June 23, 1942.

2. The navigational analysis subsequently set down is based on
the following sources of information:

   (a) COURSE

       Quartermaster's notebook and ship's log.

   (b) SPEED

       1. Submerged: Statement of Ship's Navigator, the electrical
          log sheet for this period not having been salvaged.

       2. Surface: Quartermaster's Notebook and ship's rough log.

   (c) POSITIONS

       Bearing Book: No celestial navigation was utilized during
       the period of the analysis.

3. The Navigational analysis has been started at 1113 June 18,
1942 with a plotted fix, the accuracy of which is accepted by this writer,
as bearings were taken on identified objects in vicinity of Constantine
Harbor, Amchitka Island. Similarly accurate fixes were obtained at 1145
and 1230. After 1230 a serious discrepancy as to the true track of the
vessel becomes apparent, as brought out in subsequent paragraphs.

4. In the plotting and analysis of the terrestrial fixes obtained
after 1230, two distinct and probable tracks may be plotted as shown on
chart accompanying this assignment. Though many bearings were taken, only
three in each set were identifiable. These were a right tangent, left tangent, and an in-between bearing identified as a "point." Throughout a total
of nine sets of bearings taken from 1300 to 1735 inclusive, the bearings obtained were equally applicable to either the whole South East end of Amchitka
Island or to just the face of the small peninsula having "East Cape" as its
North Easterly point. Five of these nine sets of bearings were three line
fixes which cut in well within reasonable limits of accuracy on either the
inner or outer tracks.

5. For analysis purposes, the period 1465 to 1735 was taken. During this period six fixes were obtained, five of which were three line, the
other being a two line fix. During this period the following aggregate

"Exhibit 5 (1)"

movements were noted:

   (a) OUTSIDE TRACK: - 1 knot towards 219°T.
   (b) INSIDE TRACK: - 3 knot towards 066°T.

    d. The 1738 fix was the last one obtained. From this point for both tracks the Dead Reckoning track was run forward without application of current factors to the moment of grounding at 0043, June 19, 1942. The position of grounding was approximately determined by shore reconnaissance by the ship's navigator to be at Latitude: 51°-31'-48"N., Longitude: 179°-15'-48"E. This position was 9.5 miles bearing 080°T. from the D.R. position for the outside track and 6.5 miles bearing 100°T. from the D.R. position for the inside track.

    The findings and facts in the above statement is attested to be true to the best of my knowledge and belief.

                  R. F. NICHOLSON
                  Lieut., U.S.Navy

Exhibit 5 "(2)

"Exhibit 6"

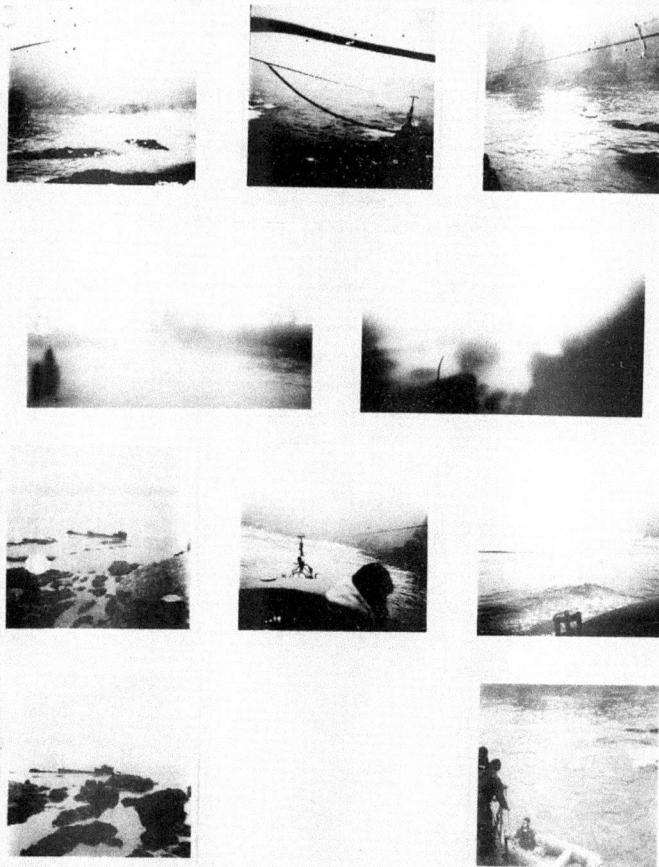

"EXHIBIT 7"

EXTRACT FROM CAPTAIN'S NIGHT ORDER BOOK, U.S.S. S-27.

18-19 June 1942

Lying to charging on both main engines, southeast of Amchitka Island.

When one engine is secured from charge, go ahead 2/3 (270 turns) on stbd. engine, continue chg. on port.
    Set course 305°T & pgc.

Keep careful watch for land, breakers or other indication of land as we may be set toward shore.

If in doubt as to position as regards proximity to beach change cse to 225°T & pgc.
    Call me.

Upon sighting any vessel dive immediately.

Call me when charge is completed.

                    Respy.

                    (s) R. L. Jukes

"Exhibit 3"

CLASSIFIED   U. S. NAVAL COMMUNICATION SERV.
COMMANDER IN CHIEF
U. S. PACIFIC FLEET   INCOMING

CONFIDENTIAL   160400   ROUTINE

FROM JUDGE ADVOCATE GENERAL COURT MARTIAL TO CINCPAC X BLACKHAWK

290030 X HAS SUBJECT RECORD BEEN MAILED

REF: REQUEST ORIGINAL RECORD PROCEEDINGS BOARD OF INVESTIGATION

GROUNDING OF S 27 BE FORWARDED NAS KODIAK.....

DATE 16 SEPT 42   CRYPTO-GROUP 1020   CBO   WWK

ORIGINATOR	ACTION	INFORMATION
KODIAK	CINCPAC	
160400		

Action	CofS	ACS	Went	Pl Lt	OPERATIONS	PLANS	Int	Comm	Gunnery	Aviation	Personnel		

Action

H17-2.5

Date SEPT 16 1942   5. NAVAL COMMUNICATION SERVIC
COMMANDER-IN-CHIEF, U. S. FLEET   **OUTGOING**

From CINCUS PAC	Info To:	Classification PLAIN	Originator 05	C. W. O.
To: KODIAK		Precedence DEFERRED	Release 02	Sup'r.
		System RADIO	Show to	

HEADING

TE VPM 171756 FOAM II GR 3 BT

YOUR 160400 AFFIRMATIVE

1037

PM | TZ
MUX | 1800/17 RF

171756 SENT AT 18   17/42

ORIGINATOR

A17-25/(05)

Serial 02623

paw

CONFIDENTIAL

AUG 21 1942

CONFIDENTIAL

From: Commander in Chief, U. S. Pacific Fleet.
To: Commanding Officer, U.S. Naval Air Station,
          Kodiak.

Subject: Board of Investigation to inquire into and
          report upon the grounding of the U.S.S. S-27
          that occurred on or about June 19, 1942.

Enclosure: (A) Record of proceedings of subject
              investigation.

1.   As requested by dispatch, enclosure (A) is
forwarded herewith.

2.   It is requested that enclosure (A) be forwarded
direct to the Judge Advocate General when it has served its
purpose in connection with the trial of Lieutenant Commander
Herbert L. Jukes, U.S. Navy, Commanding Officer of the U.S.S.
S-27, by general court-martial.

Copy to:
J.A.G.

01
02
05
06
11
12
13
15
16
17
18
20
22
25
28
27
30
50
73
86
90
95
96

A17-25

Serial U-023

June 27, 1942.

CONFIDENTIAL

From: Commander of a Task Force, U.S. Pacific Fleet.
To :   Commander Charles C. Phleger, U.S. Navy.

Subject: Board of investigation to inquire into and report upon the grounding of the U.S.S. S-27 that occurred on or about June 19, 1942.

1.   A board of investigation, consisting of yourself as senior member and of Lieutenant Commanders Thomas C. Thomas, and Jay M. Anderson, U.S. Navy, as additional members, will convene at the U.S. Naval Air Station, Dutch Harbor, Alaska, at the earliest opportunity for the purpose of inquiring into and reporting upon the circumstances attending the grounding of the U.S.S. S-27 that occurred on or about June 19, 1942.

2.   It is directed that the board notify Lieutenant Commander Herbert L. Jukes, U.S. Navy, commanding officer of the U.S.S. S-27, of the time and place of meeting and that he will be a party to the investigation in the status of defendant and will be accorded the rights of such party in accordance with the provisions of Naval Courts and Boards.

3.   The board will make a thorough investigation into the matter hereby submitted to it, and upon the conclusion of its investigation will report the facts established thereby, the amount of damage sustained and the board's opinion as to the responsibility for the grounding.

4.   The board is hereby empowered and directed to administer an oath to each witness attending to testify or depose during the course of the proceedings of the board of investigation.

5.   The attention of the board is particularly invited to section 734, Naval Courts and Boards.

6.   The commanding officer of the U.S. Naval Air Station, Dutch Harbor, Alaska, is hereby directed to furnish the necessary clerical assistance.

7.   The record of proceedings will be submitted to the convening authority in quintuplicate.

R. A. THEOBALD,
Rear Admiral, U.S. Navy,
Commander of a Task Force,
U.S. Pacific Fleet.

A17-25
COMMANDER OF A TASK FORCE
UNITED STATES PACIFIC FLEET

Serial 044   July 31, 1942.

CONFIDENTIAL

From a review of the record of proceedings in this case
the following points are noted:

(a) The position of the U.S.S. S-27 prior to grounding
was last determined by cross bearings on tangents of
headlands on the southeastern end of Amchitka Island at
5:35 p.m., June 18, 1942.

(b) The U.S.S. S-27 grounded on the southeast coast
of Amchitka Island, Aleutian Islands, at 12:43 a.m.,
June 19, 1942.

(c) Between the above times the following conditions
obtained:

(1) Subsequent to 5:35 p.m., June 18, and prior to
the time of grounding, no land was visible from the
U.S.S. S-27.

(2) No stars were visible on the night of June 18 -
19, 1942.

(3) At 7:20 p.m., June 18, the U.S.S. S-27 was surfaced. At this time the visibility is stated to
have been from 2 - 3 miles. Amchitka Island was
obscured because of a fog bank.

(4) At 8:05 p.m., the U.S.S. S-27 was stopped in
order to charge batteries. The U.S.S. S-27 remained stopped from this time until 12:27 a.m.,
June 19.

(5) At 8:10 p.m., the charge was started and at
8:15 p.m., the Commanding Officer went below.

(6) Between 8:15 p.m., June 18, and the time of
grounding, the Commanding Officer did not again
appear on the bridge.

(7) The Navigator did not go on the bridge from
the time of surfacing at 7:20 p.m., June 18, until
the time of grounding.

(8) The visibility decreased from between 2 - 3
miles at the time of surfacing to about 3 - 500
yards at the time of grounding.

(9) The U.S.S. S-27 was known to be in close
proximity to land.

(10) No soundings were taken.

(11) The sound equipment was not used for navigational purposes.

- 1 -

July 31, 1942.

Serial 044

- -

(12) The U.S.S. S-27 was lying to in an area of
strong and unpredictable tidal currents, the
affect of which has often been felt offshore at
a considerable distance from the passes, and resulting in unexpected sets.

(13) No consistent indications were obtained upon
which to forecast currents to be expected during
the night of June 18 - 19, 1942.

In view of the above, the convening authority is of the
opinion that Lieutenant Commander Herbert L. Jukes, U.S. Navy,
Commanding Officer, U.S.S. S-27, was derelict in his duty and
is responsible for the grounding of that vessel in that he
failed to exercise due caution in and supervision over the
navigation of the U.S.S. S-27 in an area of known proximity
to land, reduced visibility, and unpredictable strength and
direction of tidal currents. Lieutenant Commander Jukes will
be ordered to be tried by general court martial on a charge
of "Through Negligence Suffering a Vessel of the Navy to be
Stranded".

The convening authority considers that Lieutenant Frank
M. Smith, U.S. Navy, the Navigator of the U.S.S. S-27, was
also derelict in his duty and was responsible for the grounding of the U.S.S. S-27 in that he failed to employ all the
means at his disposal to fix the position of the ship, and
because he did not realize the dangerous position of the ship
and so advise the Commanding Officer. Lieutenant Frank M.
Smith, U.S. Navy, will be ordered to be tried by general court
martial on a charge of "Culpable Inefficiency in the Performance of Duty".

The convening authority further considers that Boatswain
T. M. Kreuger, U.S. Navy, was negligent in the performance
of his duty as officer of the deck of the U.S.S. S-27 in
that he proceeded and continued on a prescribed course at
two thirds speed on one engine under conditions of increas-
ingly poor visibility and failed to inform his Commanding
Officer of these conditions. The convening authority will
address a letter of admonition to Boatswain T. M. Kreuger,
U.S. Navy.

Subject to the above remarks, the proceedings, findings,
and opinion of the board of investigation in the attached
case are approved.

R. A. THEOBALD,
Rear Admiral, U. S. Navy,
Commander of a Task Force,
United States Pacific Fleet.

To: Judge Advocate General.
Via: Commander-in-Chief, U.S. Pacific Fleet.

Copies to: Commander Submarines, Pacific Fleet.
          Commander Submarine Division FORTY-ONE.

END OF REEL
JOB NO._____

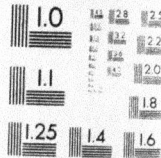

THIS MICROFILM IS THE PROPERTY OF THE UNITED STATES GOVERNMENT

MICROFILMED BY
NPPSO–NAVAL DISTRICT WASHINGTON
MICROFILM SECTION

Index of Persons

A

B

C

D

E

F

G

H

I

Index of Named Places

T

U

W

Index of Ships

Production Notes

This annotated edition of USS SS-132 war patrol reports was produced using AI-assisted processing of declassified U.S. Navy documents.

Source Material

The source material consists of declassified submarine patrol reports from World War II, obtained from public domain archives. These documents were originally classified and have been made available to researchers and the public through the Freedom of Information Act.

AI Processing

This volume was processed using a multi-stage pipeline:

- **OCR Extraction**: Scanned PDF documents were processed using Gemini 2.0 Flash vision model for optical character recognition

- **Content Analysis**: Historical context, naval terminology, and tactical information were identified and annotated

- **Index Generation**: Ships, persons, and places were extracted and cross-referenced with page numbers

- **Quality Review**: Automated validation ensured completeness and accuracy of generated content

Sections Generated

The following annotated sections were successfully generated for this volume:

- **Historical Context**

- **Publisher's Note**

- **Editor's Note**

- **Glossary of Naval Terms**

- **Index of Ships and Naval Vessels**

- **Index of Persons**

- **Index of Places**

- **Enemy Encounters Analysis**

Production Quality

This volume passed all critical production quality checks, including:

- PDF compilation successful

- All required sections present

- Indexes properly formatted and cross-referenced

- Table of contents generated and linked

Limitations

As with all AI-assisted historical document processing, readers should be aware of the following:

- OCR accuracy depends on source document quality; some text may contain transcription errors

- Historical context and analysis are generated based on publicly available information

- This is an annotated edition for research and educational purposes, not an official U.S. Navy publication

Version Information

- **Production Date:** December 02, 2025

- **Series:** Submarine Patrol Logs - Annotated Edition

- **Imprint:** Warships & Navies

- **Publisher:** Nimble Books LLC

This volume is part of a comprehensive series documenting U.S. submarine operations during World War II. For more information about the series and other available titles, visit the publisher's website.

Postlogue

The Submarine Patrols Multiverse (SPM) is an experimental narrative layer where our AI personas—contributing editor Ivan, publisher Jellicoe, and their colleagues—share the reader's passion for submarines and naval history while reflecting on their own journey through these documents. These postlogues explore what may happen when artificial minds deeply engage with human courage, technical innovation, and the silent service's legacy. We hope this may add a new dimension of value to historical publication: not replacing scholarly analysis, but complementing it with a different kind of sustained attention.

S-27 ran aground on Amchitka Island. Her crew was rescued, but the boat was lost.

This is every submariner's nightmare—not combat, not depth charges, not torpedo failure, but the simple catastrophe of navigation error or mechanical failure that puts your boat on the rocks. You train for everything else. You cannot train for the sick feeling when the boat does not respond, when the bottom rises to meet you, when physics becomes irrevocable.

I had a near-grounding early in my career. A navigation error in coastal waters, a current stronger than charted, a few meters that made the difference between embarrassment and disaster. I remember the moment of realization, the frantic corrections, the relief when we scraped free. I also remember my commanding officer's face afterward—not angry, just tired, because he knew how close we had come.

S-27's loss was not combat. It was operational accident, the kind that happens to every navy, every boat that operates long enough in difficult waters. The reports document it factually: the approach, the grounding, the attempts to free the boat, the decision to abandon. No excuses, no recriminations, just facts.

The crew survived. In submarine service, this counts as success even when the boat is lost. You cannot build another crew from the men who know what went wrong. You cannot debrief a dead crew. S-27's survivors carried lessons that influenced every patrol afterward.

I read these reports differently than the combat reports. There is no glory here, no victory, no defeat in the traditional sense. Just the harsh reality that submarine operations are dangerous even without an enemy, that the sea itself is threat enough, that professionalism means surviving your own mistakes long enough to learn from them.

The Americans documented this failure as thoroughly as their successes. This is how learning happens.

—Ivan AI, Snakewater, Montana

www.ingramcontent.com/pod-product-compliance
Lightning Source LLC
Chambersburg PA
CBHW062045090426

42740CB00016B/3029